MW00617539

The State of My State
A native son's search for West Virginia

Selected essays from "The State of My State"
newspaper column, January 2010 to March 2013

By Sean O'Leary

MarketLab, Inc.
Harpers Ferry, West Virginia

Library of Congress Control Number: 2013937367

ISBN: 978-1-59948-430-3

Published by:

MarketLab, Inc.
935 Engle Molers Road
Harpers Ferry, WV 25425
www.the-state-of-my-state.com

Produced in the United States of America
by Main Street Rag Publishing Company,
Charlotte, North Carolina

Book design by Page Hayes
Photograpny by Misty Higgins

Acknowledgments

Many of the essays in this volume were originally published in the Martinsburg Journal by former editor, Don Smith, and by current editor, Christopher Kinsler, to whom I am deeply grateful. Others have been published in the Spirit of Jefferson, a weekly newspaper edited by Rob Snyder to whom I am equally grateful.

Thanks also to the many, many people who appear in the pages that follow. Although I may sometimes criticize them, I also believe that in their different ways they are trying to make West Virginia a better and more prosperous place.

Finally, thanks to Page Hayes for designing this volume, to Misty Higgins for her photography, and to Scott Douglass, my oldest friend, for publishing "The State of My State".

The essays contained in this volume and future State of My State columns can also be found at www.the-state-of-my-state.com.

TABLE OF CONTENTS

INTRODUCTION

Years ago I stood in a conference room on the 50th floor of the Chrysler Building in New York City looking south toward the still standing World Trade Center towers. The conference room belonged to an advertising agency that had just pitched a new campaign for a diabetes drug that my client, a large pharmaceutical firm, was about to launch. In a moment I would have to critique the campaign and the assessment would not be flattering.

My experience growing up in a fading West Virginia mill town wasn't often helpful in my job, but that day it was. The agency's images of stylish, energetic seniors cavorting happily on tennis courts, ballroom floors, and beaches were stunning, even idyllic, but they bore no relationship to life in my Ohio River town and in the nearby Appalachian hollows where diabetes was rampant and where a large share of the new drug's prospective users would be found.

Ad campaigns should be aspirational, but the agency had overshot the mark and landed in irrelevance. The designers and copywriters who were nearly all young urbanites from cosmopolitan, achievement oriented backgrounds had not been able to make the empathic leap into the geographically and culturally obscure world of Appalachia where the prevailing attitude wasn't one of achievement and aspiration as much as it was of wry acceptance occasionally lapsing into fatalism.

Michael Harrington had described that world and atmosphere in anguishing detail in his 1962 book, "The Other America" in which he wrote of Appalachia,

"Tens of millions of Americans are, at this very moment, maimed in body and spirit, existing at levels beneath those necessary for human decency. If these people are not starving, they are hungry, and sometimes fat with hunger, for that is what cheap foods do. They are without adequate housing and education and medical care…. But even more basic, this poverty twists and deforms the spirit. The American poor are pessimistic and defeated, and they are victimized by mental suffering to a degree unknown in Suburbia."

Of course, Harrington was describing extreme circumstances, which weren't shared by all or even most West Virginians. And in the decades since "The Other America" was published, the sharpest edges of material deprivation have been softened. Nonetheless, to this day West Virginia sits stubbornly at or near the bottom of state rankings for virtually all measures of wellbeing whether they are economic, medical, educational, environmental, psychological, or cultural. The progress that has been made is in large part attributable to government programs and to a lesser degree to commerce. Still, the oldest and most popular means of escaping the barrenness of Appalachian life remains emigration, which data show has drained West Virginia of at least half of the people who would have lived here had the state's population growth mirrored the nation's.

I stumbled upon that statistical oddity three years ago and it made me wonder. Is it possible that the flood of emigrants, beyond diminishing West Virginia's population, has changed the state psychologically, culturally, and spiritually as well? Is it possible that those who leave are the most energetic and entrepreneurial among us and that those of us who stay behind are more inclined to acceptance and fatalism? Certainly those who leave are younger and better educated. And might those factors at least partially account for West Virginia's chronic inability to catch up with the rest of America?

It was just speculation – a facile explanation for a large and multifaceted problem. But, it was the beginning of an ongoing exploration into my home state and the peculiar dynamics that so often make West Virginia a statistical outlier – nearly always in ways that, like my assessment of the advertising agency's campaign, aren't very flattering. In fact, beyond being a statistical outlier, West Virginia is often downright paradoxical; a place that often seems to operate countercyclically to the rest of America and sometimes counterintuitively as well, making nonsense of conventional methods for understanding how people, societies, and economies work.

How can a state that has fewer working adults than any other also have an unemployment rate that's below the national average? Why does West Virginia's economy sometimes seem comparatively prosperous, but only when the economies of all the other states are in decline? Why, if the coal industry is the engine that drives West Virginia's economy, are the places where coal is mined among the most impoverished in the state and the nation? In fact, why does the coal industry, which comprises only 6% of the state's economy, loom so large in the politics and perceptions of West Virginia?

Why do the people of West Virginia cling so determinedly to coal mining jobs which may sustain them financially, but which also destroy them sometimes suddenly in apocalyptic explosions and sometimes slowly and agonizingly through black lung disease and broken bodies? Why do we blow the tops off of our mountains?

Why does West Virginia's latest putative economic savior, the natural gas industry, grow robustly while having little measurable impact on jobs or local economies? Why, when West Virginia's extractive industries prosper, don't West Virginia residents prosper as well?

Why in a state that relies more than any other on the federal government for incomes and healthcare do West Virginia's political leaders ridicule Washington for its profligacy and rage against perceived federal intrusions? Why when statistically West Virginia stands to gain more from Obamacare than any other state, are state leaders at best ambivalent about taking advantage of the opportunity? Why does West Virginia have the highest rate of death by drug overdose in the nation?

Why when violent crime has been plunging for more than a decade in the rest of America has it been going up in West Virginia? Why, when in the aftermath of mass shootings that have made the rest of America more receptive to gun control measures, is West Virginia's legislature furiously crafting new laws to vacate gun control laws and increase gun ownership and use?

Why in a state that has the lowest average level of educational attainment in America is West Virginia cutting funding for higher education even as it sits on a billion dollars in a rainy day fund and cuts business taxes? Why when West Virginians elected senators Jay Rockefeller and Robert Byrd to a combined fourteen consecutive terms, are they suddenly poised to replace Rockefeller with a candidate who is politically and philosophically his and Byrd's diametric opposite?

Why is West Virginia sometimes called the most racist state in America when white voters there gave then candidate Barack Obama a larger share of their votes than did white voters in twenty other states?

Why do West Virginia residents, who are personally unpretentious and self-effacing, become enraged at the mere mention of the word, "hillbilly" and savage any personality foolish enough to tell a West Virginia joke or television executive foolish enough to propose a West Virginia-based reality TV show?

Why? Why? Why? The questions about West Virginia are endless – endless in number and endless in what they can reveal not just about the state and its people, but about humanity.

In the essays that follow, I try as best I can to explore the questions listed above and more besides. Still, some readers will be justifiably disappointed that more questions aren't explored, particularly about important subjects such as education and the environment. But, there will always be more to ask and to say about West Virginia … and much more to do.

Sean O'Leary
March 20, 2013

THE PLACE I LOVE

THE STATE OF MY STATE

January 15, 2010

I once read that between the years 1900 and 2000 three-quarters of West Virginia towns vanished – ceased to exist. Most were probably remote coal camps abandoned when the mines that sustained them were exhausted. We've seen photographs of the refugees: gaunt men, women, and children dressed in smudged and tattered clothing, standing in front of wood shacks, looking doubtfully at a stranger who inexplicably insists on taking a picture. And from a distance of decades we thank God their unhappiness is only a memory … except that it's not.

It's true that much of the physical pain of poverty has been mitigated, so there aren't as many heart-rending pictures. But the absence of opportunity and the accompanying loss of security and hope are still very much with us in West Virginia as is the resulting abandonment of communities and of the state by those who must concern themselves more with the future than with the past.

The statistics are stunning. West Virginia's largest cities – Charleston, Huntington, and Wheeling – have lost nearly half of their populations in recent decades. The same trend applies in varying degrees to smaller cities. And West Virginia's coalfields have also emptied as an industry that once employed more than 120,000 now employs fewer than 25,000.

Today West Virginia's economic map consists of just three islands of prosperity amid an ocean of decline. The three counties forming the hook of the eastern panhandle are one island. Monongalia County, home of Morgantown and West Virginia University, is another. And Putnam County, wedged between Charleston and Huntington, is the third. These are the only counties out of fifty-five to experience population growth in this decade.

This picture of devastation may seem surprising because, as the current economic crisis rumbles through the country, political leaders boast that West Virginia has avoided much of the damage inflicted on other states. Personal incomes and employment have remained fairly stable as have home values except in a few areas and, although the state faces a $120 million deficit next year and mounting deficits in later years, that is mild compared to the struggles of other states. But, the bad news is that West Virginia's resilience is best explained by the adage, "When you haven't risen far, you don't have far to fall."

Personal incomes have remained stable because our population is the oldest, poorest, and most disabled in the nation, which results in a disproportionately large share of our incomes deriving not from work, but from entitlements that are unaffected by the recession. Much state revenue comes from transfer payments and coal severance taxes, which are also less affected. Finally, West Virginia's housing market was depressed before the recession, so there were few new mortgages created during the period when most of the famously flawed lending practices took place.

But, while these factors insulate West Virginia against the immediate scourge, they do nothing about the more severe long-term problem. And, because no one gets rich from entitlements, to the degree West Virginia is spared from the current crisis, we're also likely to be spared from the recovery.

If the direness of this portrayal seems out of kilter with what we usually hear, it's because the media tend to focus on the present and recent past while the dynamics of degradation at work in West Virginia are gradual and epochal. Another is that politicians often emphasize the optimistic and anecdotal, particularly if they fear that the forces responsible for devastation transcend government's ability to counteract them. But, whatever the reasons, a failure to grasp the severity and nature of West Virginia's economic decline contributes to popular support for policies that would worsen it.

In the last twenty years the nation has seen a redistribution of wealth from middle and lower class households, of which West Virginia has many, to wealthy households, of which we have few. The Bush tax cuts delivered to West Virginians only 60% of the savings delivered to other Americans. Other trickle-down proposals popular among conservative populists, such as eliminating the capital gains tax and the Federal estate tax or "death tax, would follow the same pattern. West Virginians are among the least affected by these taxes and, consequently, would see the least benefit from their repeal. In fact, the death tax is almost comically irrelevant in West Virginia where it applied to only 183 households in 2008.

Repealing or cutting progressive taxes such as these would produce a "catch-22" for West Virginia. If the cuts cause deficits to grow, they must be funded by remaining taxes of which West Virginians pay a greater share. If, on the other hand, deficits are offset by spending cuts, those cuts almost certainly must come from entitlement programs and transfer payments on which West Virginians depend more than other Americans. Finally, even if the cuts were to fulfill the supply-side fantasy by becoming self-financing, nearly all of the economic growth would be realized elsewhere leaving West Virginia still farther behind.

Solutions to West Virginia's economic crisis are elusive, but surely we must begin by first recognizing the nature and severity of the crisis and then by avoiding tax policies that would do further harm. ∎

JERRY WEST AND WEST VIRGINIA'S DISEASE OF THE SOUL

December 29, 2011

Jerry West is the most famous West Virginian ever to wander from these hills. He was an all-American basketball player at WVU, the ninth greatest professional player of all time according to Bill Simmons' encyclopedic "The Book of Basketball", and he remains a literal icon of the National Basketball Association, which uses the silhouetted image of Jerry West driving hard to the basket as its logo.

Jerry West is also a tortured soul. In his recent autobiography, "West by West: My Charmed, Tormented Life" (written with Jonathan Coleman) this man who has earned virtually every reward and accolade society can offer an athlete tells us he is incapable of enjoying very much of it, that he cannot experience love in the way we all at least hope to, that he is, in short, a tortured and incomplete human being.

Although he doesn't use the term, one could say that Jerry West is mentally ill.

Does that sound harsh? Some of us, perhaps West himself, will recoil at the phrase because mental illness carries a stigma. But, it shouldn't, especially in cases where the causes are all too understandable. For West it was a father who beat – not "hit" he tells us pointedly – beat him repeatedly. Meanwhile, West's mother chose not to see the abuse taking place in their barren, wood frame house in 1950's Chelyan, West Virginia.

Afraid to go home, young Jerry would spend endless hours on a dirt-patch basketball court, shooting baskets and fantasizing about game-winning buzzer-beaters – imagined moments of triumph followed by the adulation and love he didn't find at home. West calls his relationship with basketball then and now an addiction. In therapeutic terms, he was using basketball to dissociate from his pain and its causes.

Jerry West's story of abuse and his consequent behavior is unusual only in that, in the absurd lottery that is life, his chosen means of dissociation, playing basketball obsessively, happened to intersect with a freakish athleticism to produce a magic carpet ride that took him first to college, then to the Olympics, and eventually to Hollywood, far, far away from the sources of his pain. It's the one-in-a-million coincidence of which all addicts dream as they anesthetize themselves with booze, gambling, junk food, cigarettes, painkillers, assorted drugs, and still sometimes basketball.

Although Jerry West remains emotionally damaged, he escaped at least partially. Most who are similarly afflicted don't even have that. Their lives aren't saved by miraculous coincidence and their dissociative behaviors, far from being a means to prosperity, are more likely to cripple and occasionally destroy them and sometimes their families as well. It's an important issue for West Virginia because it happens here more often than in most places.

The National Institutes of Health and Centers for Disease Control rank West Virginia among the leading states for the prevalence of depression, anxiety-related disorders, and, inevitably, suicide. We're nearly five times more likely to kill ourselves than we are to be killed by someone else. And suicide combined with accidental drug overdoses (usually prescription pain killers) kills more of us than even traffic accidents.

Of course not all premature deaths associated with mental illness are sudden and traumatic. Some play out over years of gnawing misery in the form of diabetes and heart disease – conditions often caused or nurtured by chronic apathy and disinterest in our own wellbeing. All of this results in West Virginia ranking 46th among the states in life expectancy, more than six years behind the leader, Hawaii, and only seventeen months better than last place Mississippi.

It's a crisis, yet as a state we offer little support to those in need of help. Per capita state funding for mental health care is a third below the national average and we have less than half as many psychologists, social workers, and psychiatrists per capita as our neighboring states.

Instead West Virginia has largely narrowed and recast the problem of mental illness as one of drug abuse, which it's attempted to counter it through policing and legislation designed to disrupt the illegal drug trade and punish perpetrators. However, these steps, although legitimate, address only symptoms of what is at its core a disease of the soul. The result is that, in West Virginia, prisons rather than hospitals and community-based programs are the primary repositories for many of our mentally ill while most go untreated at all.

Why do we choose not to address the underlying causes? A large part of the problem is our attitude toward mental illness. Many, including some political leaders, see depression and addiction not as illnesses, but as shortcomings of character – a lack of self-discipline, a failure of resolve, or even a dearth of religious faith – traits for which they believe people should be admonished or punished rather than treated. Even Jerry West, who has yet to escape the shadow of abuse six decades after it ended and who asks our understanding, admits that he only briefly tried therapy and quickly rejected it.

Until West Virginians dismiss the stigma surrounding mental illness and embrace depression, addiction, and other conditions as treatable diseases for which a sufficient number of qualified professionals are required, the statue of Jerry West that stands outside the WVU Coliseum will be as much a monument to West's and West Virginia's disease of the soul as it is to the athletic achievements it's meant to celebrate. ∎

OF INCEST AND AUTHENTICITY

April 3, 2010

"They are a curious and most native stock, the lanky men, the lost, forgotten seeds spilled from the first great wave-march toward the West and set to sprout by chance in the deep cracks of that hillbilly world of laurel hells … and if you yearn to meet your pioneers, you'll find them there, the same men, inbred sons of inbred sires perhaps, but still the same … they are misfit and strange in our new day."

Thus did Stephen Vincent Benet describe the people of Appalachia in his book-length poem, "John Brown's Body" that won the Pulitzer Prize for literature in 1922.

We can be reasonably sure that West Virginia Governor Joe Manchin has never read this passage because, if he had, the campaign to rescind the Pulitzer Prize would be well underway.

There are few slights of Appalachia and West Virginia that don't draw the Governor's ire. His targets have included NBC television for contemplating a reality show called "The Real Beverly Hillbillies", Abercrombie & Fitch for selling a T-shirt that featured a map of West Virginia and the slogan, "It's all relative", and even then-Vice President Dick Cheney who found himself in the Governor's cross-hairs when he remarked that he had Cheney's on both sides of his family, "and we don't even live in West Virginia."

But, does any of it make any difference? Perhaps.

A few years ago the artistic director of a major theatre told me that, if I wanted my play, "Rain in The Hollows" (since retitled "Claudie Hukill"), to be produced in New York, I should change the play's setting from the hollers of West Virginia to the west coast of Ireland. He even offered suggestions about how the play's dialogue might be tweaked … no major revisions, mind you … to lend it the necessary "authenticity".

What the artistic director didn't explain was why a change in setting unaccompanied by any change in the play's substance should make theaters and audiences more receptive. On reflection, it's fairly clear that he felt "Rain in The Hollows", a play that employs magical realism to explore the nuances of family relationships, would be more "accessible" to audiences if it were set in Ireland.

Why should that be the case? One answer is that Ireland, unlike West Virginia, has produced a stream of playwrights – Synge, O'Casey, Friel, McPherson, and others – who have written highly nuanced works in this vein, so perhaps audience members are able to relate more readily to the "Irish peasant experience" than they are to the less frequently staged, "Appalachian mountain experience".

That's the polite way to describe it. There is, however, a darker interpretation that goes like this. Audiences either can't or don't want to identify with characters whose lives they associate with ignorance, provincialism, and bigotry. In other words, audience members might not be able to get past their caricatured notions of Appalachian hill people to find their underlying shared humanity.

Whichever interpretation is more accurate, the episode reminds us that the mere mention of place can evoke waves of emotions, images, and preconceptions, a phenomenon that good playwrights use to imbue their plays with color, texture, and context without having devoting pages of dialogue to tedious description. That's a good thing, but it's a good thing that can have a distressing consequence.

Calling upon preconceptions also means calling upon prejudices. And, by willfully employing audiences' prejudices, playwrights, whether intentionally or unintentionally, validate them.

An example is the frequently produced play, "The Spitfire Grill", in which a young woman recently released from prison travels to a remote lake town in Wisconsin to start over. When we hear that the crime for which she was imprisoned was murder, we are also told that she killed her father at whose hands she was the victim of incest.

Normally this kind of revelation is the proverbial hand grenade that a playwright can't simply roll on to the stage and leave unexploded. INCEST! My God! The audience wants to know.

But, if that's not really what the play is about and the playwright needs to move on, what does he do? The playwrights of "The Spitfire Grill" (James Valcq and Fred Alley) simply added a line explaining that the young woman is from West Virginia.

Why does that simple factoid bring closure to the issue of incest …defuse the hand grenade so to speak? Because incest is what audiences expect to happen in West Virginia. No further explanation is required and, in fact, the playwrights give us none. Would further explanation have been required had the young woman hailed from New York, California, Florida, or other more presumably cosmopolitan places? Certainly.

I won't go into statistics showing that incest is no more prevalent in West Virginia than it is elsewhere, but will merely observe that the writers of "The Spitfire Grill" weren't deterred by statistics either. But, does this tiny exploitation of audience members' preconceptions do any damage? I don't know, but I wonder if "The Spitfire Grill" might have been seen by a woman I met in New York recently who, upon being told that I live in West Virginia, looked at me with furrowed brow and asked plaintively, "Why?" ∎

OUR NEGRO PROBLEM

January 21, 2010

Senator Hillary Clinton was desperate prior to West Virginia's 2008 Democratic primary. A surging Barack Obama had erased Clinton's delegate lead and shattered the aura of inevitability that surrounded her candidacy. Trying to build a firewall, Clinton turned to West Virginia.

Some commentators seized upon Appalachia's reputation for ignorance and poverty and castigated Clinton's strategy as a cynical appeal to the uninformed. "The electorate's lowest common denominator" one pundit called Appalachian voters. Others suggested a darker appeal to racism, which was thought to pervade West Virginia. So, when Clinton won with 67% of the vote, the suspicion was confirmed in the eyes of some.

"West Virginia voters revealed they are the most racist in the country", John K. Wilson said flatly in The Huffington Post.

But, if Wilson was right at the time, then white West Virginians experienced a miraculous transformation because in the general election they gave Democratic nominee Barack Obama more than 40% of their votes, a figure that exceeded Obama's share of white votes in twenty other states including two, Virginia and North Carolina, that he won. Were West Virginia's black population proportional to its size nationally, Obama might have won here as well.

While the election results exposed as myth Wilson's claims of rampant racism, stereotypes and exaggerations such as his, even grievous ones, require some basis in fact. Those facts are supplied by Dr. Henry Louis Gates Jr. in "Colored People", a memoir of his childhood in Piedmont, West Virginia.

Gates, a Harvard University professor, has written numerous books and hosts a PBS television series, but he's probably best known for last year's confrontation with a white Cambridge, Massachusetts policeman that ended up being resolved with President Obama over beers on the White House lawn.

Gates was born in 1950 when West Virginia was racially bifurcated. Restaurants, theatres, jobs, and public transportation were segregated, as was the educational system. After the Supreme Court's 1954 "Brown vs. The Board of Education" decision, West Virginia University waited until 1962 to welcome its first black varsity athlete.

Gates notes the collective impact of institutional racism and he discusses the more subtle forms of discrimination that continued after integration and to this day. But the power of his narrative is in stories about individuals and relationships damaged by a forced separateness that bred mistrust and misunderstanding, truncated friendships, smothered aspirations, and kindled a corrosive resentment on both sides of the color line.

It's stunning to think that this is the lived experience of people only in their 50's and, while racism is hardly extinct, remarkable that there has been so much improvement.

The point was driven home when, not long after reading "Colored People", I visited the National Civil Rights Museum at the Lorraine Motel in Memphis Tennessee, site of Dr. Martin Luther King Junior's assassination.

The exhibits are supplemented by a succession of closed circuit TV screens that run a continuous loop of contemporaneous newscasts ensuring that Bull Connor will turn dogs and fire hoses on peaceful demonstrators from now until eternity.

Amid those images of dignity and chaos there appeared a young Senator Robert Byrd whose luscious pompadour was even then three years out of style in New York and Washington, but not in Charleston and not at the WWVA Jamboree. His softly rounded nose and chin defeated the chiseled cracker look to which he aspired, but the pompadour was flawless, a signal as certain as Sarah Palin's dropped "g's" that its owner was a tribune of the common man … the common white man.

Byrd was a former Klansman and backslapping raconteur of the Dixiecrat persuasion. On screen he was playing the brooding Cassandra, warning of the sinister Communist hand lurking behind the troublemaking "coloreds".

Suddenly the screen cut to another image and Byrd was gone. I emerged from the museum wondering if it had been a dream and how such a man could have evolved to become what some now call "the conscience of the United States Senate". And how could we white West Virginians have evolved from enthusiastic segregationists to become an electorate that gave a black presidential candidate more than 40% of our votes?

One of Gates' stories suggests an explanation. His older brother, Rocky, then an eighth grader, had apparently qualified to become the first black student to win a Golden Horseshoe Award … the state's annual prize for achievement in West Virginia history by middle schoolers. But, Rocky was denied not by legal discrimination, which was then past, but by the personal prejudice of a school board member. The injustice was reported to Gates' father by another board member who was moved to remorse by his conscience and too much to drink.

It seems fitting, even necessary, that change began in such small, squalid ways and gradually evolved into something greater and more principled.

Robert Byrd has said that his greatest regret was his vote against the 1964 Civil Rights Act. He has since compensated mightily. Perhaps by voting for a black presidential candidate at nearly the rate of white voters nationwide and possibly in proportion to the way we would have voted for any Democratic candidate, white West Virginians have acknowledged our regret. And we and our senator, whose pompadour remains flawless, can know we have grown. ∎

OUR BETTER HALF

August 13, 2010

They are apparitions that haunt us in the vacant buildings of Wheeling and Huntington and in the empty, tumbledown houses that line the hollers of southern West Virginia coal fields. They are two million souls who were or would have been West Virginians, but who instead were sucked from the state by social and economic forces that for decades have made a mockery of the efforts of politicians and business leaders to stem the flow.

The rush of emigration is so great and so sustained that it seems natural, endemic and as uncontrollable as the weather, although it is not much discussed. It should be however, because emigration defines and shapes the economy, culture, and politics of West Virginia more than politicians, more than the coal industry, and more than the Appalachian Mountains themselves.

The numbers only begin to tell the story. In 1950 there were over two million West Virginians. One out of every 76 Americans was a West Virginian. Since then America's population has nearly doubled to over 300 million, but the number of West Virginians has actually declined by 10%. So now, instead of representing one in 76 Americans, West Virginians are only one in one hundred and seventy-six. Had West Virginia's population grown in proportion to that of the nation as a whole there would be more than 4 million of us today, but there are only 1.8 million. Where did the others go? And, more importantly, what have they taken with them?

Demographers will tell you that West Virginia is the domestic equivalent of Mexico except for the fact that the immigrants we export are legal. Of course, that doesn't mean they are any more welcome.

In the 1960's and 70's it was commonplace to hear Ohio politicians complain that West Virginia was exporting its problems north. In fact, the southern suburbs of Columbus, the state capital, sometimes felt and still feel more heavily populated by refugees from West Virginia and Kentucky than by native-born Ohioans. The same is true of Charlotte, which has traditionally had the same magnetic pull on young people in the southern part of West Virginia that Columbus had on the northern part.

But, politicians in those states were wrong to complain because we weren't exporting our problems. We were exporting our future, our best and brightest. The simple fact is that, collectively speaking, our emigrants are better than those of us who stay behind. They are younger, better educated, and more entrepreneurial. Their emigration constitutes a brain drain on a scale typical of third world countries and the consequences range from the absurd to the devastating.

It has become routine to hear our Governor happily announce that West Virginia's unemployment rate is at or below the national average. What he neglects to point out is the reason. Our success owes not to our performance in creating jobs, but rather to our astonishing ability to eliminate workers. We do it in three ways.

First, we send those who want to work but can't find jobs in West Virginia to other states. Second, some of those who remain simply stop looking for work and are, therefore, not counted among the unemployed. And third, we are the nation's leader by a wide margin in the percent of workers who have been designated as disabled and, consequently, not employable.

These trends have reached absurd proportions in the coalfields of southern West Virginia. The populations in Logan and Mingo Counties are less than half of what they were in 1950. And the population of McDowell County has declined by an almost incomprehensible three-quarters. Of adults who remain in McDowell County, half are officially disabled. Today there are only 5,500 jobs in McDowell County to support a population of 27,000. Once upon a time the population there was nearly 100,000.

But what the numbers fail to communicate is the damage done to families and to the fabric of life in our communities. When populations go into decline the corresponding decline for some enterprises is merely proportional.

A community that has three gas stations may end up with only two. But social, cultural, and entertainment enterprises often vanish altogether and that, combined with an absence of educated and able workers not only impoverishes life in those communities, but removes any incentive that individual or corporate entrepreneurs might have to locate there. When that happens, communities go into an economic death spiral such as the one that has left McDowell County with almost no private sector economy.

There are a few signs that state political leaders are beginning to recognize emigration and the brain drain as problems. A bill in the statehouse that would provide tax incentives to college graduates who remain instate. However, it will only be effective if college graduates have jobs to go to. That will require new thinking within state government in the areas of taxation and economic development to focus less on extractive industries, light manufacturing, and other traditional businesses and more on providing supportive environments and funding for small start-ups and the entrepreneurial self-employed whose services can be sold to out-of-state clients.

West Virginia has few such businesses now, so there is little political pressure within the state to develop such policies. Politicians are more inclined to do things that benefit existing constituents rather than hypothetical ones. But, for West Virginia to succeed, that will have to change. ■

WEST VIRGINIA, BODY AND SOUL

March 4, 2010

They are called "malady maps" – maps of the United States that use shading to illustrate the prevalence by state of crime, disease, natural disasters and afflictions of every type. They are human misery measured in degrees of blackness, with pure black signifying the most afflicted. And, for a bewildering litany of maladies, black is the color of that little armless frog that represents West Virginia.

Diabetes, heart disease, high blood pressure, high cholesterol, drug use (pain killers primarily), tobacco consumption and, yes, tooth loss are conditions for which West Virginia is a national leader. Among the fifty states and the District of Columbia we rank 46th in life expectancy, five years behind Hawaii. Imagine that. Five extra years, living in Hawaii. Some people definitely have it better.

And it's not as though the brevity of our lives is offset by their quality. According to the Census Bureau West Virginians between the ages of 22 and 64 are the most likely in the nation to be disabled and the margin of our lead over second-place Mississippi is a staggering four percentage points.

In one sense it's not surprising that a state with a high prevalence for any one of these medical conditions should also rank highly for the others since many of them are biologically related. But they bear one other distressing relationship. They are all in varying degrees conditions of choice – conditions whose presence or severity is caused or exacerbated by the ways in which we choose to live.

I say this as a matter of fact – not to scold or nag any more than we scold or nag family members and friends even as we watch them contribute to their own destruction. Of course, we worry about them and sometimes may even risk a comment. But, most of the time we watch in respectful silence accepting "Dad" for who he is, reasoning that he knows the implications of his actions and it's his life to live …or not live, as he chooses.

Still, we must ask why we West Virginians are demonstrably less interested in living than other Americans.

As the nation's poorest state, any explanation of our plight must begin with the issue of poverty and what comes with poverty – an endemic absence of aspiration or belief that we can control or significantly alter our destinies. It's a disease called fatalism and we suffer from it prodigiously. You don't need a survey to recognize that poverty wearies many West Virginians into surrendering to circumstances even as we anesthetize ourselves with painkillers, cigarettes, and Ho Ho's …sometimes the only luxuries we can afford.

Inculcation in that barren attitude begins at a young age. At first it's almost romantic. As teenagers an absence of expectations allows us to be easy and carefree. But, by middle age it looks more like carelessness and, by old age, it morphs imperceptibly into powerlessness and resignation – the disease of the soul.

In search of an antidote, I turned to a friend who grapples with the disease daily. She is an elementary school teacher who retains her passion after years of working with children who come from difficult circumstances.

She told me about two of her students, a boy and a girl who show promise. But, when I asked about their futures, her face darkened. So, I asked what it would take to nurture their promise. What enables some kids from challenging backgrounds to transcend their circumstances while others are consumed by them?

In answer my friend smiled wanly and suggested without much confidence that they might be aided by the presence of an adult who has hope and aspiration for them – a parent, a relative, a friend …herself? But, she is clearly someone who has tried many times to share her hope only to see it fail to take hold or worse, to take hold briefly and then be gradually destroyed by the corrosive drip of day to day life.

Still, she is a romantic for whom hope and aspiration are easy to expend even when they are dashed, as they regularly are, because they are richly, outrageously rewarded when they are realized. And, though poor, wouldn't we be better and happier having had hopes that are crushed or frustrated, than to have never had them or to have never tried? Can't we always carry hope, especially for our children?

Oscar Wilde said, "We are all in the gutter, but some of us are looking at the stars." Those who are looking at the stars may suffer from many maladies, but not from the disease of the soul. ■

WEST VIRGINIA'S GUN PLAGUE

January 26, 2013

It's odd that in our debate about guns and killing we rarely mention the form of death in which guns are most frequently involved. It's not murder or acts of self-defense, which serve as the usual bookends of the argument. It's suicide.

Even if you add all of the murders, all of the killings that take place in self-defense, and all of the accidental deaths in which guns are involved, you don't come close to matching the number of times someone puts a gun to his head or heart and pulls the trigger.

The fact is, when guns kill, the victim is usually the gun's owner.

This is disturbing because, when the perpetrator and the victim are the same person, slogans such as, "The only way to stop a bad guy with a gun is a good guy with a gun" become nonsensical. We're forced to transcend simplistic notions of "good guys" and "bad guys" and enter the real and messy world of personal strife, pain, and struggle.

So often we hear that law-abiding gun owners are trained in how to use guns properly. But, what we need to know is are they trained to cope with the wounds and pain and disappointments that life inflicts and that drive people to deranged actions?

They demonstrably are not. The states that rank first, second, and third for gun ownership – Wyoming, Alaska, and Montana – also rank first, second, and third for suicide. West Virginia, which ranks fifth in gun ownership, is only seventeenth for suicide, but even that rate is a quarter higher than the national average.

Of course, the risks associated with guns don't end with suicide. There are murders, most of which are committed, not by strangers or intruders, but by family members on one another or by people with whom the victim has a close relationship. At the time they purchase guns people almost never do so with the expectation of killing themselves, a family member or a boyfriend or girlfriend. But, that's what happens.

Simply stated, when you introduce guns into your home, you may or may not reduce the threat of being attacked or killed by an intruder – the statistics on this point are vague – but you unquestionably increase the risk of major injury and death to yourself, family members, and guests.

In a 2006 paper in the New England Journal of Medicine, doctors Matt Miller and David Hemenway showed that people living in homes with guns are twelve times more likely to suffer violent injury or death from that weapon than they are from the actions of an intruder. Moreover, men in the states with the highest rates of gun ownership are four times more likely to commit suicide with a gun than their counterparts in the states with the lowest rates of gun ownership. And women in high-ownership states are eight times more likely than their counterparts to kill themselves with guns. The added risk extends to children as well.

That's why some of us look askance at claims that gun ownership is an effective method of self-protection.

And it's not as though the carnage of suicide and domestic violence can be fobbed off on the entertainment industry, which has become the NRA's latest scapegoat as it tries to deflect attention from guns. While video games and movies glamorize depersonalized violence and mass killing, the same is not true of suicide, which is almost never depicted, or domestic violence, which, even when depicted, is rarely glamorized.

It's simply the case that the suddenness and near certainty with which guns work make them perfect tools for impulsive acts of suicide and murder.

But, there's some good news. Nationally rates of firearm-related crime have dropped over the past twenty years, as have rates of gun ownership, which is down to less than a third of American households.

Unfortunately, this has not been true in West Virginia where gun ownership remains over 50%. West Virginia used to be the safest state in the nation, but is no longer. Over the last fifteen years, as the nation's murder rate has dropped by a third, West Virginia's has risen by 14%. As a result we now rank 24th, tied with New Jersey and ahead of New York. And, for every murder in West Virginia, there are more than three suicides, which puts us way ahead of both New York and New Jersey in total deaths by firearm.

We also spread the plague. On a per capita basis, West Virginia exports more guns that are used in crimes than any other state.

Still, the NRA and others who oppose virtually all efforts to control guns fall back on the second amendment guarantee of the right to bear arms – a right that they argue is necessary so that an armed citizenry can dissuade or defeat would-be tyrants who would seize the government.

But, no right is absolute. And our democracy's bulwarks against tyranny are the Constitution's guarantees of basic rights and the voice in government bestowed on all citizens. Against those noble guarantees, quaint notions of tyrannical government take-overs being repulsed by armed citizen insurrectionists are trivial and come at the price of 19,000 suicides a year, a murder rate three times that of Canada and four times that of the UK, and, of course, Columbine, Aurora, and worst of all, Sandy Hook. ∎

WEST VIRGINIA'S MISSING UPPER CLASS

August 25, 2012

The phrase, "upper class", is provocative. Among conservatives it's heard as an alarming call to class warfare. Among liberals, particularly those sympathetic to the "Occupy" movement, "upper class" is shorthand for the oligarchical 1% that they believe controls America's wealth and institutions.

The substitute phrase, "rich people" or simply, "the rich", is almost as provocative, which is why Republicans in congress have banned it and replaced it with the pleasantly scented, "job creators", a euphemism of startling inaccuracy that reminds us that the point of euphemism is to mask unpleasantness even at the price of distortion.

But, whether you call them "the upper class", "rich people", or "job creators", there is one abiding fact – West Virginia doesn't have many of them. This isn't an ideological point. It's a statistical one.

Consider that if you were to equalize the population of Connecticut, the nation's wealthiest state, with that of West Virginia, the poorest or next-to-poorest state, Connecticut's richest 1% of households would have as much income as West Virginia's richest 22%. If you don't bother equalizing the populations and simply take them as they are, just the top 2% of Connecticut households, about 27,000 families, have an aggregate income equal to that of all of West Virginia's 750,000 families.

The implications of this inequality are profound economically, socially, and culturally. And they should be politically, but strangely are not.

The presence of the wealthy and very wealthy creates demand for products, services, cultural and educational opportunities, entertainment, and even environmental conditions that have a beneficial halo effect for those who live in their proximity. Restaurants, theaters, schools, galleries, and retail stores contribute to vibrant and diverse communities. Even though most of us cannot afford to take advantage of these opportunities as often as the wealthy, we can afford to do so sometimes and wouldn't be able to at all if it weren't for the regular patronage of the well endowed.

The presence of wealthy people also tends to produce a cleaner, healthier environment and those in their proximity enjoy the benefits as well, which is among the reasons that the wealthy and those around them have noticeably longer life spans.

This isn't to say that all good things derive from rich people or that their presence has only good effects. But, we need look no farther than West Virginia to see the kind of society that their near absence creates.

In contrast to the diverse and vibrant places in which the wealthy reside, West Virginia is economically, culturally, and socially bland and depressed.

When people describe West Virginia as being unusually homogeneous they're usually making reference to our lack of racial diversity. But, they could just as easily be talking about the age distribution of our population, which is concentrated in early old age, educational attainment, which is concentrated at the high school level and below, cultural and artistic opportunities, of which we have the fewest in the nation, and our environment, which is among the nation's most toxic.

The result is a comparatively barren place that is first and foremost an industrial zone in which the presence of people is tolerated, but only so long as they don't complain about toxins in their environment or interfere with corporate interests. It's not surprising that wealthy people almost invariably choose to live elsewhere.

West Virginia's lack of wealthy residents also has political implications. One of the great political battles currently raging in Washington and between West Virginia's congressional candidates is whether the Bush-era tax cuts for those making more than $250,000 a year should be extended.

Republicans including Senatorial candidate, John Raese, Congressman David McKinley of West Virginia's first district and Shelley Moore Capito of the second, say they should. Democratic Senator Jay Rockefeller and Congressman Nick Joe Rahall of the third district say they shouldn't. Meanwhile, Senator Joe Manchin wanders in his usual fog of political calculation.

What's fascinating is that West Virginia's lack of wealthy residents makes the outcome of the debate almost irrelevant to the state. With only a little more than 1% of West Virginia families making more than $250,000 a year, not many will be affected by the tax cut, nor will West Virginia's economy. We are far more likely to feel the effects of the drawbacks if the reduction is extended. The federal deficit will increase as will pressure to cut federal entitlement programs upon which West Virginia is more dependent than other places.

On the other hand, in Connecticut, where more than 10% of families make more than $250,000, the benefit of the tax cut for the wealthy will be much greater. For every dollar the average West Virginia family saves as a result of the tax cut extension, the average Connecticut family will save $10. And for every dollar that the tax cut pumps into West Virginia's economy, Connecticut's economy will receive $22.

This means that the already doubtful and factually unsupportable claim that reducing taxes on the wealthy fuels job and income growth for working Americans is being replaced by the even more laughable claim that cutting taxes on rich people in Connecticut will generate jobs and income in West Virginia.

A few years ago Thomas Frank wrote a book, "What's the matter with Kansas?", in which he wondered why Kansans, who are famously conservative, consistently vote for candidates whose economic policies put Kansas at a disadvantage. The same question should be asked of West Virginia's Republicans in congress. ∎

WEST VIRGINIA NEEDS A NEW PARADIGM

March 13, 2012

It's over. We lost. Royal Dutch Shell announced that its nearly mythical ethylene cracker plant is going to Pennsylvania.

Shattered are our hopes for 12,000 new jobs. Shattered also should be the myth that cutting and abating taxes is an effective strategy for attracting businesses and revitalizing West Virginia's economy.

But, that's not all. The loss of the cracker should also cause us to reassess not just the ways in which we try to accomplish economic prosperity, but whether it's even possible for West Virginia to do so and, if it's not, ask what other more attainable and perhaps better goals we should pursue.

If that sounds defeatist, look at the facts. West Virginia has never – not from the day it was created – been prosperous. Due to a decades-long tradition of emigration by the young and educated, we have the poorest, oldest, least educated, unhealthiest, most disabled population in America. We lack any major commercial or population centers and, with the exceptions of the eastern and northern panhandles, we have no proximity to any. We have only one major education center, which not coincidentally is one of our two tiny islands of prosperity, the eastern panhandle's Washington DC exurbs being the other.

For the most part, we are a cultural desert, a fact I would not have thought quantifiable until stumbling across a National Endowment of The Arts analysis of census data, which showed that West Virginia has the fewest working artists per capita of any state. Finally, much of what would otherwise be valuable virgin forestland is despoiled by coal mining, an industry that discourages the development of other industries and produces economic misery everywhere it is present.

That's a great deal to overcome when trying to attract new residents, businesses, and investment – also things in which we trail the nation. Nonetheless, we've recently invested a great deal of hope in natural gas, both its extraction and in the industries it can spin off, which brings us back to the cracker plant.

If discounting the state could be a winning strategy for West Virginia, we would have won this one. We offered Shell $300 million in tax incentives, which would have created what Ted Boettner of the West Virginia Center on Budget and Policy called "a virtual tax-free environment". It's as though Governor Tomblin hauled the state to the end of the driveway like an old commode, spray-painted it with the word "FREE" in day-glow letters, and then watched Shell drive on by.

Why?

First, as big as $300 million in tax breaks sounds, it constitutes only about a 1% reduction in the future plant's operating costs – not that big of a deal just as tax breaks generally are not that big of a deal. Second, numerous studies show that companies' larger concerns when building or relocating are the availability of an educated and skilled workforce, a strong supplier base, transportation and communication infrastructure, and attractive communities – things West Virginia struggles to provide.

But, can't we invest in better educating our children, retraining our workers, making ourselves healthier, and building better infrastructure? The answer is, yes, we can and we should. But, we shouldn't expect those efforts to produce economic prosperity, at least not as it's conventionally defined.

All the time we're educating our children and retraining workers, most will still not be able to find jobs commensurate with their skills and knowledge in West Virginia. Many will migrate to other places leaving us still with a comparatively poorly educated and older workforce.

But, maybe that's OK.

Maybe West Virginia needs to change the paradigm for what constitutes success. Maybe the best thing we can do is educate our children and all West Virginians excellently and prepare them to achieve personal prosperity even if they find it elsewhere. After all, isn't that how most West Virginians already define success within the context of our own families?

We raise our children hoping they'll go to college and expect them afterward to seize opportunity wherever it arises – probably out of state. When they do, we count it as success. So, why shouldn't the state adopt that same outlook even if the results don't show up in standard measures of economic performance?

Maybe West Virginia needs its own standards, new standards focused on human outcomes rather than state outcomes. What would the new metrics of success be if the state adopted the same aspirations as its families and devoted its resources to supporting them? How would our taxing and spending priorities change?

These are important questions because success defined as economic prosperity may be unobtainable for West Virginia by any means and our current strategy of tax cutting achieves neither that goal nor any other. So, perhaps it's time to change the goal.

We could do worse than to be the state that, like a family, takes care of its own, prepares its children well, and willingly sends them into the larger world ready to achieve success. And, if we do that, we'll probably find that gradually even traditional measures of economic performance will improve as well – a nice bonus, but by then, it won't matter nearly as much. ■

WEST VIRGINIA'S COAL TATTOO

A RAGE NOT FELT

April 26, 2010

"In the big world the old people do be leaving things after them for their sons and children, but in this place it is the young men do be leaving things behind for them that do be old."

So says a bereaved mother lamenting the loss of a son in John Synge's play, "Riders to The Sea". But, it's a lament that could have been uttered by mothers of coal miners in Farmington, Sago, and most recently Upper Big Branch where families lost the bet that a $20 an hour pay check could compensate for the ever-present risk of death.

It's a gamble requiring a calculus familiar to those who wrestle with the paradox that the means by which they gain their livelihoods may also kill them. And make no mistake, all who enter the mines do the calculus.

At one time we all did because in nature sustenance always comes at the risk of death. It's a measure of civilization's progress that most of us are spared from that paradox. So, from the safety of our insulated lives, we watch with compassion but also curiosity the anguish of the Upper Big Branch families whose plight is ancient and strange to us now. And, try as we might to be with them and support them, we know we are not of them and we are grateful.

Of course, miners are not the only ones who do the calculus. Others include regulators and mine owners among whom none is more accomplished than Don Blankenship, CEO of Massey Energy, owner of the Upper Big Branch mine. The fact that Massey's stock price has not dropped catastrophically since the disaster is evidence of Blankenship's acumen. He didn't know the disaster would happen, but he knew it could and that it was cheaper to invest in liability insurance than in changes to the mine that might have prevented it.

Still, Blankenship can be forgiven for saying that nothing is more important than miner safety. Such statements are and are understood as expressions of sentiment rather than of fact. The question is whether Blankenship even shares the sentiment. It's doubtful.

According to "The State Journal" the Mine Safety and Health Administration "issued 48 withdrawal orders in 2009 at the Upper Big Branch Mine for repeated significant and substantial violations that the mine operator either knew, or should have known, constituted a hazard." Meanwhile, Massey mines were placed on potential "pattern-of-violation" status 13 times since 2007, more than one third of all such citations in the industry. But, what's damning is Blankenship's attitude toward enforcement of safety regulations. In 2007 Massey contested 97% of the major safety violations at the Upper Big Branch mine.

Finally there was the news conference at which Blankenship was asked about the implications of the Upper Big Branch disaster. Pivoting neatly on the graves of his dead employees, he used the occasion to bemoan the possibility of more federal regulation, something he self-assuredly asserted, "no one wants."

No one? Really? Are we that helpless, that cowed? Would we hold harmless a company whose negligence may have caused miners' deaths rather than risk the loss of jobs? Is our fear so reflexive that we've forgotten basic economics which teaches that, if the mine has value and we drive out Massey, a new owner will step forward to preserve jobs and almost certainly be more committed than Massey to safety since they could hardly be less so?

Sadly, the answer to these questions may be, yes. And the sadder truth is that some no longer have to suppress rage before acquiescing because they no longer feel rage at all … so conditioned have they become.

We are complicit in a system that often allows malefactors to "pass along to consumers" the costs of their misdeeds, which brings to mind Benjamin Franklin's observation that those who give up liberty to obtain a little safety deserve neither. Isn't justice as precious as liberty and might not the same be said of it?

It's an infuriating tradeoff in this day of populist outrage. But, even populism is strangely directed anymore. Ten years after deregulated energy markets produced the Enron meltdown that plunged thousands into financial ruin and two years after nearly unregulated financial markets destroyed wealth and jobs on a scale not seen since the Great Depression, the fear voiced by our most active populist group, the Tea Party movement, is not that there will be too little government regulation, but that there will be too much.

Of course, Blankenship did that calculus as well. He and fellow directors of the U. S. Chamber of Commerce donated a million dollars to the Tea Party movement among whose organizers is former Congressman Dick Armey who was a driving force behind both energy and financial deregulation and whose Institute for Policy Innovation received $200,000 from Enron.

Maybe that's why at recent West Virginia Tea Party events, there wasn't a sign condemning Blankenship or Massey. Quite the opposite, Blankenship is an invited speaker at Tea Party rallies.

So, as miners do the calculus they must every day, Tea Partiers can lash our President and other suspected socialists to a post and follow Don Blankenship and Dick Armey who will direct the formation of a circular firing squad before retreating to the safety of their corporate board rooms from where they will give the order to fire, aim being unimportant. ■

WEST VIRGINIA'S COAL TATTOO

January 27, 2012

A lyric from Johnny Staats's song, "Coal Tattoo" goes like this —"Somebody said, 'That's a strange tattoo you have on the side of your head.' I said, 'That's the marking of the number nine coal. A little bit more 'n I'd be dead.'"

The tattoo mentioned in the song title is the indelible mark left when coal shards penetrate skin, injecting a black so pure that it appears blue against flesh. It's a mark shared by West Virginia miners and figuratively by all of us who live in this state where coal isn't just a commodity and a source of jobs, but a social, cultural, and psychological phenomenon. In large measure, coal is our identity.

To an economist unfamiliar with coal's cultural and social significance this would come as a surprise because coal is neither West Virginia's largest industry – healthcare, manufacturing and trade are bigger – nor its largest employer.

Coal mining accounts for just 6% of West Virginia's gross domestic product, 6% of wages, and 3% of jobs. Even if we squint to see coal's impact on downstream and supplier industries, the share of jobs and wages rises to just 8.7% and 10.7% respectively.

Most people, both inside and outside of the state, assume coal's significance to be many times that. The mistake is understandable though because we're saturated with impressions of coal – from politicians' rhetoric and images of the tops blown off of mountains to industry advertising and simple legend.

In popular myth coal is synonymous with West Virginia and its stature remains undiminished from past decades when the industry employed six times the number of people it does now and accounted for 20% of GDP. But, that was long ago. So, why has the coal industry's influence in state government remained strong, even dominant, while its economic significance has plunged?

Coal's leverage derives first from the disproportionate share of state and local taxes the industry pays. Although coal delivers only 6% of GDP, its share of state taxes is two to three times that much making coal more important to politicians than to residents or businesses. And, although coal mining occurs in just twenty-six of West Virginia's fifty-five counties, those counties are highly dependent on property taxes paid by the industry, which in some places amounts to a third or more of total receipts.

As congressional donor lists reveal, coal also donates heavily to politicians and causes. Even West Virginia's congressional districts – especially our tortured second district – are configured so that all are anchored in coal country. And in Charleston and southern West Virginia, coal's influence is pervasive in the legal profession and among suppliers of professional services.

Political influence is important to the industry because its economic and environmental effects on the state and communities are at best problematic. A recent report by the West

Virginia Center on Budget and Policy determined that the state spends more to support coal than the industry pays in taxes. Meanwhile, the impoverished conditions of counties where the industry is most active are legendary and not merely coincidental.

Whereas most businesses prefer to operate in prosperous, growing communities, affluence and population growth pose problems for coal by driving up property values and raising demands for a clean environment and high standards of living and of public health, issues with which the industry struggles. In short, aside from a shared interest in keeping the lights on, coal mines and people do not coexist happily.

In this and in other ways the coal industry is an economic dinosaur – primitive, large, and not easily adaptable to a diverse modern society and economy. Even the marketplace in which coal companies operate is unique.

Most businesses must compete on multiple fronts – price, quality, innovation, customer service, and labor and material cost among others. But, coal is a commodity, so prices are rigidly set by the market with little or no opportunity for product innovation or differentiation. That's a disadvantage economically because it precludes the kind of success that companies in other industries achieve by introducing breakthrough products and services. But, it's helpful politically because the lack of multifaceted competition among coal companies produces a commonality of interest that encourages them to unite in political activism – which they do aggressively and successfully.

Strangely though, political factors – the EPA, global warming, and safety regulation – are not coal's most immediate threats. The Wall Street Journal recently carried a story calling 2012 a "grim year" for coal, saying, "The two biggest threats facing U.S. coal companies are the low price of domestic natural gas, which is making thermal coal a less-attractive fuel for their utility-customers, and the shaky economic picture in Europe, which is damping exports of metallurgical coal." This past week "The Economist" magazine seconded that opinion and pointed to longer-term trends that signal the decline of coal.

For West Virginians who expect natural gas to be our financial savior it must be jarring to read that salvation, if it comes, will be at the expense of coal.

Still, for the reasons cited above, the coal industry's political influence will probably remain disproportionately strong even as its economic contribution inexorably shrinks. Sadly that influence will probably divert attention and resources from other more promising and badly needed opportunities.

As Senator Robert Byrd wrote in 2009, "West Virginians can choose to anticipate change and adapt to it, or resist and be overrun by it." ∎

BLACK LUNG AND THE GHOST OF WALTER REUTHER

July 21, 2012

Initially I saw no connection when a Google search popped up a new documentary film about a former Wheeling resident and, on the same day, The Center for Public Integrity and National Public Radio reported a resurgence of Black Lung disease.

But, in the days following, as I waited for Governor Earl Ray Tomblin and Senator Joe Manchin, both of whom profess unending concern for the welfare of miners, to react to the news that black lung may be more prevalent now than it was forty years ago, a connection between the seemingly unrelated events emerged.

When I was thirteen years-old Wheeling's Oglebay Institute purchased the old Zion Lutheran Church for the purpose of converting it into Towngate Theater. Today Towngate is one of America's most venerable community theaters. It has produced hundreds of plays and thousands of actors, at least two of whom have gone on to win Academy Awards. But, in 1969, it was a rundown shell and the challenge of renovating it fell to my dad, Hal O'Leary.

One day, while we were hauling out rubbish, my dad called me into a little storage room where he had found an old church register. He said, "Look at this", and pointed to an entry.

There were the names, "Mr. and Mrs. Valentine Reuther", followed by those of their children, Victor, Roy, and Walter.

"What do you think of that?" he said. I looked at him blankly.

Dad was appalled by my ignorance and, after wondering aloud, "What do they teach you in that school?", he told me about Walter Reuther.

Although he would die in a plane crash a year later, Reuther was then and since 1946 had been the president of the United Auto Workers union. But, more than that, he was an architect of twentieth century America.

Reuther practically invented employer-provided health insurance, making it a standard feature of full-time employment. He was also a primary force behind minimum wage laws, overtime pay, paid vacations, and pensions for hourly workers.

Reuther marched arm-in-arm with Martin Luther King, with whom he shared the podium the day King delivered the "I have a dream" speech. He marched again with King from Selma to Montgomery and, when Walter Reuther died, King's widow, Coretta Scott King eulogized him as, "a crusader for a better world" who "was there when the storm clouds were thick."

Along the way Reuther survived two assassination attempts and accusations that he was a communist and a traitor. But, he prevailed and in 1995 was posthumously awarded the Presidential Medal of Freedom by President Bill Clinton. In 1998, Time Magazine named Reuther one of the 100 most influential people of the 20th century. And President Ronald Reagan paid homage to Reuther when, upon enactment of legislation creating Employee Stock Ownership Plans, he cited Walter Reuther as the bill's inspiration.

The compelling story is told in a new documentary, "Brothers on The Line", directed by Walter Reuther's great nephew, Sasha Reuther.

So, Reuther's ghost haunted me as I wondered when our governor and senator would respond to the news that Black Lung Disease is 50% more prevalent now in southern West Virginia than it was nationally 40 years ago. It's a scourge that has killed at least 75,000 miners and, more frightening, its presence was recently found in the autopsies of 17 of the 29 miners killed in the Upper Big Branch explosion in 2010. They were already dead men walking.

Inevitably I wondered how Reuther, who had to lead often bloody strikes to earn union recognition, would react if his union members were being killed.

Certainly not in the fashion of Manchin and Tomblin – Tomblin, who in the aftermath of the Upper Big Branch mine disaster, loudly signed into law what he called "monumental" mine safety legislation that did almost nothing.

As reporter Ken Ward Jr. of the Charleston Gazette points out, Tomblin's "monumental" law failed to require real-time ventilation and monitoring of coal dust, the cause of the Upper Big Branch explosion. The bill's "new" rock-dust standards are redundant having already been enacted two years earlier. An "anonymous mine safety tip line" announced at the bill signing was also already in existence. A new requirement that miners be tested for drugs addressed an issue that's peripheral at best and which had nothing to do with the Upper Big Branch explosion or any other mine disaster. And the bill's increased fines for safety violations were actually watered down by Tomblin's administration and are, in any case, lower than those in federal law.

It seems that in West Virginia, it isn't just Walter Reuther's church that has been replaced by theater. His fight for the workingman has been as well.

Finally, a spectacularly ill-timed attempt by Republicans in the House of Representatives to reduce Black Lung enforcement roused Manchin from his stupor. He opposed the attempt, but did so without acknowledging the black lung report.

"We should never go backward when it comes to the health and safety of our miners", Manchin said.

Earth to Joe, "We already have."

Tomblin, meanwhile, is mute. I should probably stop waiting for him to don the mantle of Walter Reuther whose vigilance once earned him a would-be assassin's bullet. Earl Ray isn't about to take a bullet for anybody. Probably the most we can hope for is another Academy Award performance. ∎

THE REAL WAR ON COAL

May 7, 2012

Much is made of President Obama's and the Environmental Protection Agency's "war on coal". And it's true. In order to reduce air pollution and retard global warming, this administration, along with the governments of nearly all industrialized nations, is trying to reduce the burning of coal for the generation of electricity.

But, how much of a difference are the president's policies making on the amount of coal that's mined and on the number of jobs in the mining and power generation industries? In fact, let's ask the big question. If this president is swept from office in November and the EPA's power to regulate carbon dioxide emissions is removed, as presumed Republican challenger, Mitt Romney, has said he would do, what would it mean for America's coal industry?

Would there be a rebirth? Would coal-burning power plants that are currently slated for closing become viable again? Would new coal-burning power plants be built to meet the growing demand for electricity? Would mines that have been closed be reopened? And would there be a rebound in hiring creating thousands of new jobs in the mining industry?

If you believe that the answer to any of these questions is, yes, you haven't been paying attention to the market forces that, far more than government action, are killing coal in general and the Appalachian coal industry in particular.

What are those market forces? First, there is natural gas.

If the Obama administration is conducting a "war" on coal, then the English language hasn't invented a word of sufficient ferocity to describe the conflict between coal and natural gas. Although West Virginia politicians are loath to admit it, every new gas well that's sunk in West Virginia is another nail in the coffin of coal. Why?

The practice of fracking has greatly increased supplies of natural gas and reduced the price to the point that it costs only half as much to generate a megawatt of electricity from natural gas as from coal – half as much.

That's warfare. And, in case you're under the delusion that the competition between coal and gas is friendly, consider that between 2007 and 2010 Aubrey McClendon, CEO of Chesapeake Energy, the largest gas driller in West Virginia, donated $26 million to the Sierra Club's campaign to block the construction of coal-fired power plants. Just last month McClendon did a victory dance when a Wall Street Journal writer asked him about his reputation as "the scourge of coal". McClendon said, "I probably am not as strident as I used to be because I don't have to be. Natural gas has won in the marketplace and it is continuing to win."

Far more than the president's "war on coal", the natural gas industry's war has had measurable effects. Last year the amount of the nation's electricity generated by coal dropped by 8.9 percent and coal is now responsible for less than 40% of the electricity generated in the US. This was partially attributable to warmer-than-average winter weather, but the bigger factor was natural gas, which saw its volume grow by 7.2 percent.

And natural gas's price advantage isn't going away anytime soon. One of the reasons gas is so cheap is that the "wet gas" found in many of the Marcellus shale wells in West Virginia, also produces byproducts such as ethane, which is used in the plastics industry. At current prices, these byproducts almost double the value of natural gas. Economically this functions as a subsidy for which coal has no answer.

The second market force crushing coal in Appalachia is cost. The volume of Appalachian coal produced per miner dropped by 25 percent between 2001 and 2008. This decline in productivity is driven by the exhaustion of easily accessible coal seams and produces higher costs and reduced competitiveness in the face of the onslaught by natural gas.

The third market force killing coal is the American people.

In its April issue, Mother Jones magazine ran a story by Mark Hertsgaard documenting the virtual moratorium that has fallen upon the construction of new coal-fired power plants, particularly in the eastern part of the country. While there are just over 30 new coal-fired plants currently under construction in the US, more than 160 have been blocked often by local residents who don't want what they perceive as a dirty industry in their back yards. They look not only at the global warming impact of coal burning, but at its effect on health as measured in elevated levels of asthma attacks and death.

By the end of the decade these combined market forces will have produced almost twice as much of a reduction in carbon emissions as would have been achieved under the proposed (and, in West Virginia, the much-reviled) cap and trade legislation that died in 2010.

Does that mean that Obama administration actions on coal are irrelevant or superfluous? Not altogether. Clean-air regulations are causing some older coal-fired power plants to be taken offline sooner than they otherwise would be because it's not worth the cost to retrofit them with pollution control equipment. However, this is only slightly speeding up the inevitable. Those plants, like the coal industry as a whole, are dead men walking, not because of government action, but because of the free market. And the question for West Virginia's political leaders is whether they will finally focus on building a post-coal economy rather than trying to postpone the inevitable. ∎

WEST VIRGINIA'S DEAD CAT BOUNCE

June 11, 2012

Here's how it would be written if it were a play. Governor Earl Ray Tomblin gets the latest report from the federal Bureau of Economic Analysis and happily discovers that West Virginia ranked third among all states for economic growth in 2011. While he basks in the glow of the wonderful news, his secretary of commerce enters and announces that over the past three years the coal industry added more than 1,500 jobs!

Oh joy beyond joy!

The governor, who is running for re-election, can barely contain his glee as he dictates a press release boasting, "West Virginia's strong growth in Gross Domestic Product indicates our state is on the right economic path." But, what he really looks forward to is the hellacious party he's going to have with his buddies in the coal industry, which accounted for more than 80% of West Virginia's growth.

When he arrives at the party, he bursts into the room holding up champagne bottles in each hand and shouts, "Gentlemen, your business and my re-election chances are better than ever!"

And he waits for the cheers to wash over him …and he waits …and he waits, until finally, mercifully, a glum-faced coal executive says, "Earl Ray, let me explain something to you."

"The only reason our sales went up is because we stopped trying to compete with natural gas and then we raised prices on all the poor bastards who can't make the switch.

"You understand, Earl Ray? We didn't mine more coal. We mined less. And we can only charge these prices until our remaining customers build new power plants or refurbish old ones to run on natural gas, which is what I guarantee you every one of them is doing."

The bewildered governor is confused. "But, you're hiring new miners."

The coal executive rolls his eyes. "Dang it, Earl Ray. Don't you understand anything? I told you. We're taking advantage while we can and it's not going to be for long. Yeah, we're hiring new miners, but productivity is dropping faster than green grass through a goose, which means our costs are going up just as fast. And when the cost gets as high as the price, which it will, pfffft!"

The governor: "Pffft?"

The executive: "Yeah. Pfffft! As in game's over."

The governor: "Do you mean like overnight?"

The executive: "No, there will always be a few who will keep their coal-fired plants online because they can't afford to build something new. And then there's metallurgical coal."

The governor: "But that's …that's …"

The executive: "That's not much. Are you beginning to understand now? All that growth and those jobs you're bragging about. It's what the folks in market research call a dead cat bounce.

The governor: "I'm a dog man, myself."

The executive: "Then you should appreciate this. You know how, if you throw a dead cat out of an upstairs window, it bounces a little when it hits the ground? Well, that bounce doesn't mean it's coming back to life and this little economic bounce you're so worked up about doesn't mean coal's coming back either. In fact, it means exactly the opposite.

The governor: "But, this isn't going to happen before the election, is it? You know, pfffft?"

The executive: "No, you're good until the election Earl Ray. The Bureau of Economic Analysis won't issue its next report until next June. And even that one probably won't be so bad, but a couple of years from now ..."

The governor: "It'll be bad, huh?"

The executive: "Don't worry. Coal mining only accounts for about 3 percent of the jobs in West Virginia anyway. Besides, you're the master of managing the unemployment rate. If jobs leave the state, just send the workers along with them. And, if the workers won't go, get them to file for disability. That'll keep your unemployment rate down just fine. West Virginia's made it work that way for decades."

The governor: "But what about my press release? I said the state's on the right economic path."

The executive: "It's all right, Earl Ray. Manchin, Caperton, Wise, Underwood, Rockefeller, and Moore all said the same thing and it worked out for them. So, take your press release and go on out there and toot your horn all you want. And remember, if anything really bad happens, just blame it on the EPA." ■

COAL WAS WEST VIRGINIA

December 3, 2010

Weren't those commercials in which Joe Manchin put a bullet through the Cap and Trade Bill cool? Isn't it neat that John Grisham's bestselling novel, "The Appeal", was based on a coal company CEO's attempt to buy a Supreme Court seat right here in West Virginia? And don't you remember back in the sixties when WVU football could be heard on radio and every commercial break featured God's own choir on loan to Consolidation Coal Company singing the glorious refrain, "Coal is West Virginia!"?

As recently as last month an editorial in this newspaper declared, "No other issue even approaches the importance of coal for West Virginians."

That's a very large claim to make about a state that has the nation's lowest average income, the highest rate of disability, the lowest level of educational attainment, the highest prevalence of half a dozen diseases, as well as the highest rate of death by drug overdose.

Of course, some people will argue that the revenue West Virginia earns from coal is critical to addressing these challenges, while others will argue that coal is a cause, either directly or indirectly, of many of them. And both groups have some justification. Either way, the issue of coal still rises to the top reminding us that our embrace of coal was always a Faustian bargain.

We've always known that the thing which sustained us was also killing us and, thus, in addition to all its other roles, coal became our greatest source of drama and pathos. From the coal wars of the 1920's, so effectively memorialized in John Sayles's movie, "Matewan", through assorted strikes, a murder of a union president and his family, the Buffalo Creek flood in which 125 people died and more than four thousand homes were destroyed, and including any number of mine explosions and cave-ins always accompanied by days-long vigils marked by hope and nearly always a tragic ending, coal has been the beginning and the end, the alpha and the omega.

It was all summed up neatly by Mother Jones, the union organizer who famously declared, "When I get to heaven, I shall tell God Almighty about West Virginia" – and, of course, she was talking about coal.

So, it is with a touch of regret, but also with overwhelming relief that I, a native son of West Virginia, steeped in its history and mythology, am here to tell you that coal is dead. And the sooner we begin thinking and acting as though we're a post-coal state in a post-coal economy, the better off we'll be.

When did coal die? It's hard to fix a precise date. Certainly a line was crossed at some point as the number of coal mining jobs in the state declined from 130,000 in the 1940's to only 20,000 today. It could have been when the number of disabled miners first surpassed the number of working ones. Or maybe it was when we started blowing the tops off of our mountains to get at the stuff. But, more likely it was when coal fell to only fourth place as a contributor to the state's gross domestic product behind government, manufacturing, and healthcare. Shall we have the choir sing, "Medicare is West Virginia"?

In fact, today coal generates only 9% of West Virginia's GDP even if you include all of its supplier industries. The number is just 6% if you confine the analysis to the coal industry itself. And only three West Virginia households in a hundred have a worker in the coal industry. Finally, this year the West Virginia Center on Budget and Policy released an analysis showing that the cost to state government to support the coal industry actually exceeds the amount the industry contributes in taxes and fees.

But, the most withering fact may be that where there is coal there is misery. The West Virginia counties that are most dependent on coal are also West Virginia's poorest and those which are losing population the fastest.

Perhaps it would be different if the wealth extracted from our soil stayed in the state and in those nearly shuttered coal communities that are increasingly populated only by the old and infirm. But, less than 5% of West Virginia coal is mined by West Virginia-based companies. So, a few of us get paychecks and the state gets some taxes, but the profit, the big money, goes elsewhere.

What did the editorial say? "No other issue even approaches the importance of coal for West Virginians." Maybe that was true once, but no longer.

Coal is now West Virginia's issue of mass distraction, commanding more attention and more public resources than its contribution warrants. That's dangerous because, whether Cap and Trade comes to pass or not, coal's value to West Virginia will continue to decline and, as it does so, those who are most dependent on coal will clamor even more loudly for West Virginia to increase subsidies to an industry on which the rest of the world is turning its back.

More and more effort for fewer and fewer returns. It's a game we can't win and hopefully our leaders won't try. Instead, they must begin to develop a vision and strategy for a post-coal West Virginia.

What will that West Virginia look like – maybe Vermont with a twang? I don't know. But, as I compare that state's economy with ours, it doesn't sound so bad. ∎

THE EMPEROR HAS NO NATURAL GAS BOOM

CURSED — WEST VIRGINIA'S MARCELLUS SHALE

December 19, 2011

With the recent enactment of rules regulating the extraction of natural gas from Marcellus shale, a process known as "fracking", some believe West Virginia will experience an economic boom. Newspapers have called our Marcellus shale deposits "a godsend" and Bill Maloney, the recent Republican candidate for governor, described them as "the biggest opportunity for lasting growth and prosperity that West Virginia has seen in decades".

Since "lasting growth and prosperity" is a phrase not often associated with West Virginia, it's understandable that the subject of fracking has commanded the governor's and legislature's obsessive attention for the past few months.

But, what if it's not true? Set aside for a moment the real and legitimate environmental concerns surrounding fracking. What if the gas drilling boom isn't an economic game-changer for West Virginia?

To understand why it might not be, let's visit the African country of Angola, a nation of 19 million people most of whom live in grinding poverty. Two-thirds survive on incomes of less than $1.70 per day. Most are illiterate and average life expectancy is only 40 years.

This would be just one more heart-rending story from a hellish place were it not for the fact that Angola is the world's fourteenth largest exporter of oil generating $3,600 annually for every resident. It's also the world's fourth largest exporter of diamonds and has other abundant mineral resources. In short, Angola is figuratively and literally a goldmine.

So, with lots of income and abundant resources, why are Angolans so poor and what does it have to do with us?

West Virginia is the Angola of the United States. West Virginia coal generates almost $11 billion in sales annually – $6,000 for every person in the state. Yet, we have one of the nation's lowest median incomes and staggering rates of poverty. While state GDP has increased in the last decade, population and wealth have barely budged. And the economic scourge is worst in places where coal is most prevalent – the southern counties whose economy has retreated to a nearly pre-industrial state and where average life expectancy is ten years below the national average.

Both Angola and West Virginia suffer from what economists call a "resource curse" – a phenomenon in which, for structural reasons, vast holdings of natural resources fail to translate into prosperity. This has been true of West Virginia and coal for a century and will probably be true of gas as well. Here's why.

First, most of the wealth generated by gas won't go to West Virginians. As with coal, almost all of West Virginia's gas will be extracted by out-of-state companies that will repatriate the profits elsewhere.

Second, the royalties West Virginia residents will receive won't be overwhelming. Do you remember Senator Joe Manchin dismissing the recent payroll tax cut as being paltry because it saved West Virginia families only $14.50 a week – so little "they probably don't know they're getting it"?

Guess what. That insignificant $14.50 a week translates into $750 million annually. At current market prices and assuming royalties equivalent to 20% of the selling price, even if gas sales increase at a compound rate of 13% annually, they won't generate $750 million annually until 2017 and won't equal the accumulated value of the payroll tax cut until 2022.

That kind of growth is still good and welcome, but not transformative. However, even those growth rates may not come to pass.

Drillers pump when the market price gives them an incentive to do so and, because gas is a commodity, prices fluctuate greatly. As Europe and Asia begin tapping their large shale gas reserves, supplies will increase and prices may drop. If so, production and royalties in West Virginia will drop as well.

It may be argued that this overlooks two other important benefits of the gas boom – job growth and severance taxes that will help balance the state budget.

Dr. George Hammond, associate director of the West Virginia University Bureau of Business and Economic Research, recently projected that job growth in natural resources and mining will slow significantly. He explained, "Lower coal production in West Virginia translates into coal mining job losses during the next five years. However, the job losses in coal mining are expected to be offset by job gains in oil and gas extraction."

In other words, we'll be treading water. And did you notice that, as gas grows, coal declines? The dynamic isn't just coincidental. Future growth in gas depends in part on its ability to replace coal as a base fuel, which for West Virginia means that as one hand gives the other takes away.

Finally, gas drilling's contribution to the state budget through severance taxes will be offset in large measure by added costs for inspectors and the maintenance of roads and infrastructure necessary to the industry. In fact, if gas turns out to be like coal, the costs may equal or exceed the tax revenue.

The most likely outcome of West Virginia's natural gas boom will be the enrichment of a small number of property owners and industry workers, a burst of revenue and expenditures for the state, but, little change from the depressed status quo for most West Virginians.

Of course, we can always hope for "lasting growth and prosperity" from gas, but first we'll need Harry Potter to remove the resource curse. ∎

DISCOUNTING OUR WAY TO PROSPERITY

February 14, 2012

By the time this column is published we may know whether Royal Dutch Shell has awarded West Virginia the much discussed ethane "cracker" plant that brings with it the promise of 12,000 high-paying jobs. It's a prize badly needed in West Virginia and one that has rightly concentrated the minds of the governor and legislature, who have put together a tax reduction package worth more than $300 million in an effort to lure the plant.

The $300 million figure was arrived at by Sean O'Leary in an analysis published by the West Virginia Center on Budget and Policy. (Note: The "Sean O'Leary" who authored the WVCB report and the "Sean O'Leary" who writes this column are different people.)

In his report O'Leary argues that the cost to the state and localities of providing the tax breaks is not trivial because the facility will create additional need for public services. Meanwhile, he says there is little evidence that tax breaks play a significant role in determining where businesses locate.

Regardless of whether the cracker plant ultimately comes to West Virginia, the question of whether tax incentives attract businesses and jobs is important because both political parties are committed to reducing business taxes as a means of stimulating economic growth. Indeed there seems to be a consensus that through tax cuts West Virginia can discount its way to prosperity.

This year, in the face of future cost increases for entitlements and other programs, West Virginia reduced business taxes by $15 million and Republicans in the legislature want to use growing natural gas severance tax revenues to create a permanent "tax reduction fund" that would be used to eliminate the tax on business equipment and inventory. Meanwhile, we're in the midst of lowering the corporate net income tax rate from the current 8.5% to 6.5% by 2014.

It's all being done in an effort to make West Virginia more competitive as a place to do business. And there's a prima facie case for the need to do so because, West Virginia faces serious obstacles.

We have the oldest, least educated, most disabled, and most impoverished populace in the country. Cultural opportunities are few. High-speed Internet access is sporadic and our environment is among the nation's most toxic. These are serious drawbacks for companies looking to relocate.

So, we have a choice. Correct these flaws, which will be a daunting, time-consuming task requiring spending and investment. Or put the money that could be used to correct the flaws into tax cuts in the hope that potential employers can be bribed into locating here even as they hold their noses while doing so. But, are business tax cuts a big enough incentive?

It's not likely. An examination of the economics of the cracker plant illustrates why.

First, we should note that, even without additional breaks, West Virginia's business tax burden is already competitive. The Tax Foundation ranks West Virginia's business tax climate as 23rd best in the nation, substantially ahead of our primary competitor for the cracker plant, Ohio, which comes in at 39th.

Still, we have offered Royal Dutch Shell about $12.1 million per year in tax savings for the next 25 years. That sounds like a lot of money, but Royal Dutch Shell will spend $3.2 billion to build the plant and something north of $500 million a year to operate it. So, over 25 years, the tax breaks will reduce Royal Dutch Shell's operating costs by only about 1.5%, little more than a rounding error.

Meanwhile, through free market forces, West Virginia already offers much more significant cost advantages. On a position-by-position basis wages in West Virginia are 20% lower than they are nationally. For the cracker plant, that translates into a labor and supplier cost savings of more than $76 million annually –six times the amount the state is offering in tax reductions. We offer other significant market-based advantages as well.

Because these free market savings dwarf the proposed tax incentives, we have to ask ourselves whether the tax incentives are needed, or are we just leaving money on the table?

Companies deciding where to locate first must determine that there's a qualified workforce, the necessary supplier base, and a quality of life that will make their managers open to relocating. Only then do they consider operating costs of which taxes are, as we have seen, a small part. That's why, if West Virginia can meet businesses' primary needs, our built-in labor cost advantages will usually enable us to win and tax cuts won't matter.

The problem is that too often we can't meet businesses' primary needs. We're vastly undereducated. Our supplier base is not well developed. Due to geographic isolation and environmental degradation, our quality of life is not attractive. And our funding for education, especially higher education, remains low given the level of need.

Only by addressing these problems can we create an environment that's attractive to business. And the money that would otherwise be squandered on superfluous tax cuts is necessary to do that. The cracker plant may come to West Virginia, but if it does it will be in spite of the tax breaks rather than because of them. The same can be said for most business relocations.

West Virginia has been a cheap place to do business for a long time. If we could have discounted our way to prosperity, it would have happened long ago. ∎

THE EMPEROR HAS NO NATURAL GAS BOOM

December 13, 2012

On December 10th Governor Earl Ray Tomblin convened his annual Governor's Energy Summit at which leaders from industry, academe, and government gathered to studiously avoid addressing the only question that should have been on the agenda. Why has West Virginia's natural gas boom so far proven to be an economic non-event?

You remember the hype. The process known as fracking would enable drillers to tap West Virginia's vast Marcellus shale natural gas reserves generating tens of thousands of new jobs and hundreds of millions of dollars in new tax revenue that would put the state on the road to sustained economic prosperity. "Game-changing" was a favorite descriptor among politicians and pundits.

But an accidentally more accurate description was uttered when a state official called the prospects, "mind boggling". That's because a comparison of the boom's actual economic effects to those that were predicted suggests that minds were indeed "boggled".

The problem isn't that that natural gas production hasn't grown as predicted. It has. Since 2008 volume has risen by 87%. But, the jobs, severance tax revenues, and economic prosperity that were supposed to grow as well are an altogether different story.

In November Workforce West Virginia reported that since 2008 oil and gas employment has risen not by tens of thousands or even by 1,000. Just 916 jobs have been added – less than 10% growth in four years. And the severance tax that was expected to produce tens of millions of dollars in new revenue has grown not at all. Despite the huge rise in production, severance taxes in 2012 are no greater than they were in 2008.

But, if the effects on the state's economy aren't great, surely the counties where drilling is concentrated must be prospering. The State Journal recently reported that four counties – Marshall, Wetzel, Doddridge, and Harrison – account for 87% of Marcellus shale gas production in West Virginia. Are they booming?

Since 2005, just before the dawn of the Marcellus shale era, the combined populations of these four counties have grown by 1,001 people – less than 1%. The size of their workforces has actually declined by almost a thousand. And the number of jobs has dropped by more than 2,000, causing the combined unemployment rate to rise from 4.4% to 6.9%.

Yes, but we're just coming out of recession, so aren't the Marcellus counties at least doing better than the rest of West Virginia where there is little drilling activity?

No.

The rest of the state has actually experienced slightly more population growth and less job loss. And, while the unemployment rate in these four counties is half a point below the state rate, it was half a point lower before Marcellus drilling began.

In short, by every important metric, West Virginia's Marcellus shale natural gas boom has failed to produce any measurable benefit for the people of West Virginia.

Why?

It's hard to quantify the dynamics underlying a phenomenon the existence of which few are aware or willing to admit – least of all the captains of industry, government, and academe who sold us on "the Marcellus Miracle" and, in most cases, continue to believe in it. But, four factors almost certainly play roles.

First, amid the glut of inventory brought about by fracking, the price of natural gas dropped even more than the volume increased, which explains why severance taxes failed to grow. It also means that property owners' royalty checks are much smaller than they had hoped.

Second, many landowners who receive royalties don't live in West Virginia. The last study I could find on absentee land ownership was done in 1981 and, at that time, a majority of the state was owned by out-of-state individuals and corporations while 15% was owned by the government, which means that residents of West Virginia owned only about a quarter. There's little reason to think the situation has improved and much reason to suspect it has worsened.

Third, companies doing the drilling and their investors are almost entirely out-of-state entities, so any profits go out-of-state as well.

Finally, many and probably most of the drilling jobs that have been created are held by out-of-state workers.

If some of this sounds vaguely familiar, it's because West Virginia has seen this picture before. In our southern coalfields, as much as 80% of the land is owned by out-of-state interests and the historical result has been a massive repatriation of wealth that has left those counties among the poorest in the nation despite their mineral treasure.

Still, there are some flickers of hope that West Virginia's natural gas boom will not be a replay of the state's dismal experience with coal. Gas prices may rebound a little, although not to the degree that many expected even a year ago. And, as the Clarksburg Exponent Telegram recently reported, some companies are beginning to locate headquarters and natural gas processing centers in West Virginia, which may finally produce some job growth.

But, the problem of out-of-state ownership of land and production is immense and structural, meaning wealth will continue to drain from the state. For this, there is no market solution and government's ability to address the problem is limited. Yet, if the problem isn't addressed, future phases of West Virginia's gas boom may be as barren as the current phase has been.

That's why it's time for the exaggerations about the economic impact of natural gas in West Virginia to end and the hard work of finding solutions to begin. ∎

HOW WE WERE FOOLED

January 1, 2013

Thus far West Virginia's Marcellus shale natural gas boom has been a myth. While production has grown significantly, predicted economic benefits – tens of thousands of new jobs, tens of millions of dollars in new tax revenue, and hundreds of millions of dollars pumped into local economies– have failed to materialize.

Workforce West Virginia calculates the number of jobs added by the oil and gas industry since 2008 to be 916 – less than 10% growth in four years. Meanwhile, severance tax receipts haven't grown since 2008. And you don't have to be an economist to see that Marshall, Wetzel, Doddridge, and Harrison counties, which host the bulk of drilling activity, are not booming.

The question is, why? Haven't our leaders told us natural gas is a game-changer for West Virginia? Aren't they supported by studies such as the 2010 Marcellus Coalition study and most recently a report by the U.S. Chamber of Commerce's Institute for 21st Century Energy, which suggests the industry could generate 29,000 jobs by 2020 and 58,000 by 2035?

The answer is, yes, they are. So, why have they and the studies been wrong? Let's look at the reasons.

Studies are based on statistical models, which can suffer from two kinds of errors: factual and methodological. The studies upon which policy-makers have based their optimistic expectations for economic growth in West Virginia have suffered from combinations of both. Here are some examples.

Overestimating the price of natural gas. Tax revenues and royalties are determined in part by the market price of natural gas, which studies from two to three years ago typically assumed would bottom out at about $4.50/thousand cubic feet and then gradually rise to between $6 and $8.

Instead, the supply glut brought about by fracking caused prices to descend to $2 and recover only to the present level of $3.25 – far below the amount expected.

Underestimating the effect of absentee ownership. One study that overestimated economic impact in West Virginia also did so in Pennsylvania where it was shown that the authors assumed 95% of royalty payments would go to Pennsylvania residents and into Pennsylvania's economy. In fact, only 63% did so vastly undercutting the local economic impact.

Misunderstanding what people do with royalty payments. At least one major study assumed property owners would treat royalties like regular income and spend it within a year. In fact, recipients saved more than 40%, greatly lessening economic impact.

Overestimating the share of goods and services the gas industry purchases from West Virginia suppliers. These purchases drive "indirect" job growth. However, gas companies, virtually all of which are out-of-state entities, seem to be purchasing less than expected from West Virginia suppliers.

Overestimating the share of jobs occupied by West Virginians. At least one study assumed that the share of natural gas jobs occupied by West Virginians would mirror the share in other industries. This assumption seems to have been spectacularly inaccurate.

In addition to these factual errors, studies have also had methodological flaws.

Some studies get primary data from surveys of drilling company executives who report their expectations for production, purchasing, and hiring. This group, which seeks to attract investors and curry favor with politicians, tends to be overly optimistic, which may explain why many companies haven't fared any better than West Virginia. Chesapeake Energy, West Virginia's largest driller, has seen its stock price drop by two-thirds since 2008.

Finally, studies often fail to fully account for the costs of natural gas drilling. These costs offset some benefits. For instance, if a gas well that generates $10,000 in income replaces a cornfield that generated $7,500, the economic gain is only $2,500, not $10,000. Similarly, if the presence of a gas well diminishes the value of the property for commercial or residential purposes, there is also an economic loss.

Natural gas drilling also costs individuals and communities in other ways. It requires the construction and maintenance of roads and other infrastructure. Sales tax exemptions and other subsidies granted to companies can detract from economic benefit. And there's the problem of risk. Laws designed to encourage development sometimes shield companies from full responsibility for damages resulting from their activities. So taxpayers bear the costs.

These factors and the others previously mentioned have caused studies to consistently exaggerate the economic benefits of natural gas development. The effect has been compounded by uncritical acceptance by politicians and journalists who repeat the claims and, thereby, confer credibility on them.

Perhaps now that discrepancies between predictions and performance are becoming apparent, journalists will begin to question assertions of job growth and economic stimulus or at least note that previous predictions have been unduly and even wildly optimistic.

And maybe our leaders and we will adopt realistic expectations of the economic benefits. The market price of gas may never be as high as we once hoped. And the problems of absentee ownership and development are structural, which means there are no easy remedies. Consequently, whether or not the price of natural gas rises, much of the wealth that's generated will continue to drain from West Virginia.

So, while we can make things better by training West Virginia workers to fill jobs, by driving the hardest possible bargain on taxes, and by assuring that the industry shoulders the economic consequences of health and environmental risks, we should also recognize that the term, "game changer" has been and probably will always be a misleading rhetorical flourish. ∎

FANTASYLAND

ALICE'S ADVENTURES IN WONDERLAND, WV

April 9, 2012

"I can't believe that!" said Alice. "Can't you?" the Queen said in a pitying tone. "Try again. Draw a long breath and shut your eyes."

We could all use that advice when contemplating data purporting to describe West Virginia's "through the looking-glass" economy. Just as Einstein described a parallel universe in which the laws of Newtonian physics break down and all sorts of absurdities are possible, West Virginia's economy turns the laws of conventional economic understanding upside down.

If in the last few years you paid attention to the news or, better yet, to press releases from the governor's office, you would have heard that West Virginia leads the nation in personal income growth (June 2011), economic growth (October 2008), export growth (February 2012), and home ownership (for years). Meanwhile, West Virginia has the lowest incidence of underwater mortgages in the nation (February 2012) and our unemployment rate is a full point below the national average (also February 2012).

We should be bathed in prosperity. Right?

No. We're still the poorest, unhealthiest, and least livable state in the nation. That being the case, the question is how does West Virginia produce these glowing economic statistics and what do they mean?

Let's start with our below-average unemployment rate. The calculation is simple. Divide the numerator – the number of people with jobs – by the denominator – the number of people working or looking for jobs. The more people who find jobs, the lower your unemployment rate – or at least that's how it's supposed to work.

But, creating jobs is hard. So, West Virginia discovered that it's actually easier to decrease the denominator, the number of people in the workforce. How?

First, lots of West Virginians who look for work give up and move elsewhere. The result is that in the last sixty years, during which America's population doubled, West Virginia's has not changed.

Second, we disable people at a ferocious rate and, because the disabled are not counted in the workforce, West Virginia achieves the mind-bending result of having an unemployment rate that's below the national average while the percent of adults between the ages of 22 and 65 with jobs is less than in any other state.

If that sentence leaves you a little disoriented, like Alice, take the White Queen's advice and draw your breath and shut your eyes while we consider another statistic –West Virginia's leadership in personal income growth between 2008 and 2009.

At that time the nation was fully in the grip of recession. All but three states saw declines in personal income, which is made up of wages, dividends and interest, and transfer payments. The latter, transfer payments, are often referred to as "entitlements" and include unemployment insurance, Supplemental Social Security Insurance, Food Stamps, and other programs.

Because of West Virginia's historically dismal economy, wages, dividends, and interest make up a smaller share of incomes here than elsewhere. So, when the economy and those three items tanked, West Virginia was less affected than other states. Meanwhile, entitlement funding, which made up a disproportionately large share of West Virginia incomes, increased making West Virginia a winner amid a sea of losers.

In other words, West Virginia's comparative personal income performance improved as a direct result of general economic decline.

Still feeling queasy? Well, buck up because West Virginia's brief leadership in overall economic growth is similarly a case of addition by subtraction.

Because a disproportionate share of West Virginia's GDP comes from government services and healthcare, which remained fairly robust during the recession, West Virginia's GDP grew while virtually every other state's declined.

Of course, our brief leadership in personal income and GDP growth was sure to end once the nation's economy began recovering, as it did, and now West Virginia is duly reverting to its place near the bottom of the stack.

Meanwhile, West Virginia's leadership in housing – a highest-in-the-nation rate of home ownership and lowest-in-the-nation incidence of underwater mortgages – is an example of the adage, when you haven't risen far, you don't have far to fall.

Home ownership rates have always been high in West Virginia because the state is rural, housing prices are low, and because West Virginia offers few opportunities to economic immigrants who seek jobs and who make up a large share of the nation's rental population. At the same time, because most of West Virginia never experienced a boom in housing prices, there was no bubble to burst when the market crashed in 2008. So, few mortgages were susceptible to going underwater.

But, at least West Virginia's leadership in export growth in 2011 is good news – as far as it goes. Unfortunately, it doesn't go far.

Last year West Virginia exports increased by 39%. However, the growth came entirely from the coal industry and that would be fine except for two factors.

Because the vast majority of coal exported from West Virginia is owned by out-of-state companies, the profits from increased shipments are largely repatriated elsewhere. And, because the coal industry employs only about 20,000 West Virginians, the impact on jobs and wages is small.

It's just one more case of prosperity in the mining industry failing to translate into prosperity for West Virginians. And it's one more way in which West Virginia's "through the looking-glass" economy makes absurdities of standard measures of economic performance.

Or, as the White Queen might say of West Virginia's economy, "Jam tomorrow and jam yesterday, but never jam today." ∎

THE DELUSION OF "UNLEASHING CAPITALISM"

August 23, 2012

In 2007 then West Virginia University economics professor Russell Sobel published "Unleashing Capitalism: Why prosperity stops at the West Virginia border and how to fix it".

Professor Sobel's book was a hit. Copies were mailed to every state legislator. Sobel was invited by then Governor Manchin to address his cabinet as well as a joint session of the senate and house finance committees. The state Republican Party chairman described "Unleashing Capitalism" as "our party platform".

The book's policy prescriptions are simple.

- Lower taxes and regulations including lowering or eliminating the business franchise tax and personal tax on inventory, machinery, and equipment.
- Reform West Virginia's courts to reduce the number of suits against businesses and the size of awards.
- Limit the growth of state government.

Some of these recommendations are being implemented. The Manchin administration initiated across-the-board business tax cuts that are continuing under Governor Earl Ray Tomblin. And, while there has been no significant progress in the area of tort reform, an effort to limit the size of state government is underway.

Governor Tomblin's administration is grappling with an anticipated $400 million shortfall in next year's budget and the only solutions floated thus far involve cutting state services. No political leader of either party has suggested that some of the impending deficit be addressed by deferring or reversing reductions in business taxes which, when fully implemented, will cost the state over $200 million annually.

That's because Unleashing Capitalism's thesis that cutting taxes and reducing the size of government will spur economic growth has become an unquestioned article of faith. Some legislators even carry copies of the book with them the way sixties radicals carried Mao's Little Red Book.

The problem is, in almost every major respect, Unleashing Capitalism's analysis is wrong and the effects of its policy prescriptions are not those claimed by professor Sobel.

Sobel's argument is that the more "free" an economy is, the more prosperous it will be. In his parlance, "free" means minimal taxation, minimal regulation, and a minimal role for government in society.

The evidence for this claim is a body of research conducted by the Fraser Institute that periodically scores state and national economies for degrees of economic freedom and then ranks them by per capita gross domestic product.

Report after report shows that as economic freedom increases, so does GDP. The reports also show that West Virginia, the poorest or next-to-poorest state, has "the least-free market economy in America".

But, when the Fraser Institute's criteria for measuring "degrees of freedom" are examined, what emerges is a flawed methodology that conflates causes with effects and employs criteria that have more to do with ideological preferences than they do with "freedom".

A prime example is the report's first major criterion – "the size of government", the smaller being the better. Size of government is measured by the percent of GDP taken up by government expenditures, transfers of income and subsidies, and Social Security payments.

The problem is that the share of the economy comprised by these items is more likely to be the result of private sector performance than its cause – a fact demonstrated by the 2008 financial collapse. Government expenditures for unemployment compensation, Social Security, and other programs grew in response to the private sector slowdown, which is what they were supposed to do. By performing this useful function, these programs helped prevent the slowdown from descending into full-on crisis as occurred in the Great Depression. But, according to the Fraser Institute, they simply made our economy "less free".

If the same logic were applied to the question of how we should overcome illness, we would conclude that, because sick people use more medications than those who are well, the medications must be the cause of their illness and they should stop taking them.

By conflating cause and effect Sobel's claim that "free economies" are more prosperous becomes a meaningless self-fulfilling prophecy. Further evidence is provided by another report.

Every year, The Tax Foundation, a conservative, free market-oriented organization, ranks the tax environments for business in the various states. Unlike the Fraser Institute, the Tax Foundation report focuses exclusively on something that lawmakers control – tax rates.

This year West Virginia's tax environment ranks twenty-third in the nation. We can add to that ranking the fact that in the last six years West Virginia has offered additional targeted tax incentives ensuring a virtual tax-free environment to almost any employer prepared to bring a couple of hundred jobs.

Yet, how many companies have come? Very few and, in those six years, the actual number of employers in West Virginia has actually declined.

Why?

Because, contrary to what Sobel implies in "Unleashing Capitalism", cutting business taxes doesn't make much of a difference. The one or two percent savings in operating costs the tax cuts represent are too small to change employer behavior and in any case are dwarfed by the real financial incentive West Virginia offers employers – wages that are almost 20% below the national average.

That's why, if discounting could bring prosperity to West Virginia, we'd have it already.

Cutting business taxes is politically easy and "Unleashing Capitalism" gives doing so a veneer of respectability. But, the facts reveal it to be nothing more than an economically and intellectually bankrupt way of avoiding the hard work that's necessary to attract business to West Virginia – educating our work force, building modern infrastructure, and cleaning up our environment. ■

FANTASYLAND, WEST VIRGINIA

March 4, 2013

According to his office's press release West Virginia Attorney General Patrick Morrisey sent a letter to President Obama on February 11th "expressing his concerns about the current direction of the Environmental Protection Agency (EPA), and urging the President to change the agency's "current path" by nominating a more reasonable successor to recent EPA Administrator Lisa Jackson". As an example of the EPA's unreasonableness, the highly publicized letter cited the agency's "delay in issuing a permit for a West Virginia mining site" which, "resulted in the layoff of nearly 150 workers".

The problem is that it wasn't true. There was no layoff, a fact revealed not by a reporter or a news organization. It had to be pointed out by a guy named Rob Goodwin in a letter to the editor in the Charleston Gazette.

Sadly, gaps between rhetoric and fact, like the one in Morrisey's letter, are commonplace in West Virginia – in its politics, in its news reporting, and in its lawmaking.

One of the few journalists to readily acknowledge the problem is Ken Ward, Jr. of the Charleston Gazette. Ward recently issued a series of tweets bemoaning the frequency with which lawmakers make unsubstantiated claims and are assisted by reporters who echo the claims, neither demanding sources nor checking the facts. So, when at a recent hearing on reforming the procedures under which teachers are hired and fired, Senator Bob Plymale claimed that grievance judges almost always side with seniority, Ward tweeted to a reporter covering the hearing, "Does he have data to support that?"

Of course, Plymale didn't.

Meanwhile, Ward has shown us how it should b done. Last year, in the wake of the Upper Big Branch mine tragedy, Governor Earl Ray Tomblin signed a "monumental" mine safety bill, which, a Ward story revealed, did almost nothing. The law didn't require real-time ventilation and monitoring of coal dust, which caused the UBB explosion. "New" rock-dust standards were redundant having been enacted two years earlier. An "anonymous mine safety tip line" was also already in existence. A requirement that miners be tested for drugs addressed an issue that has never been tied to a mining disaster and which had nothing to do with the UBB explosion. And the bill's increased fines for safety violations have not been implemented to this day.

It's important to note that Ward's story wasn't an "opinion piece". It didn't stake out a position either "for" or "against" the law. Nor was it really an example of "investigative journalism" since the facts contained in the story required only a comparison of the new law's provisions to existing state and federal law. The story was simply a solid piece of reporting that presented the new law in the context of the facts. And they, not Ward's opinion, undercut the governor's claim that the law was "monumental".

Sadly, Ward's work is a rarity. Consequently, we're regularly confronted with bogus claims and heavily hyped, but vacuous pieces of legislation that attract fawning press coverage with nary a trace of analysis.

Since 2010 West Virginia has been cutting corporate income taxes ostensibly to stimulate job growth, but with no quantitative evidence that jobs have been added. Meanwhile the state will lose over $191 million in revenue by 2017 and now faces the prospect of painful budget cuts.

Similarly, West Virginia hands out roughly $100 million annually in corporate tax incentives, loans, and grants without any analysis of their effect. Only every three years does the Commerce Department provide the legislature with a report and even there it omits the names of recipient companies, the size of their incentives, and any results that have or have not been achieved.

Then there's the EPA's supposed "War on Coal", which is widely believed to have cost West Virginia thousands of jobs. Yet, there is no data to support the claim, nor is the absence of that data often reported. Meanwhile, there is abundant data showing that massive miner job losses have resulted from automation, the increased use of strip mining and mountaintop removal, and, most recently, the emergence of inexpensive natural gas as a competitor to coal. But, state leaders would rather blame the EPA and reporters let them.

Similarly, the natural gas boom is regularly said to be creating tens of thousands of jobs in the state. At last count fewer than a thousand jobs have been created and there has been no measurable increase in economic activity or employment in the counties where drilling is most prevalent, all facts which are almost never noted in stories about "the boom".

Finally, the governor is considering whether West Virginia should expand Medicaid under Obamacare. He publicly wrings his hands over the costs to the state, which are almost never quantified. Meanwhile, he and the press regularly fail to mention the $600 million in federal funds that expansion will inject every year into the state's economy.

In short, West Virginia is often an accountability-free zone where content-free politicking combines with fact-free news coverage to produce impact-free laws – laws that may appeal to public sentiment, but which accomplish little or nothing often at the price of draining the state of resources.

Former Defense Secretary, Donald Rumsfeld, observed that there are known knowns, known unknowns, and unknown unknowns, but in West Virginia we're also afflicted with knowable unknowns and we're afflicted with them because we're just too lazy to ask or, better yet, demand. ∎

THE DEFINITION OF A SCHMUCK

December 5, 2012

An old joke tells us, "Only schmucks pay retail", a humiliation you know if you've had a vacation ruined by some twerp sitting next to you at a cruise ship bar delightedly boasting that he paid only half of what you did for the cruise. Sometimes schmuck abuse is elevated to a moral principle. I used to have a boss who would raise prices on foolish clients – charging "stupid fees" he called it – on the grounds that doing so reallocates money to those who use it wisely – meaning himself – thereby increasing economic efficiency.

But, to be a really big schmuck, that is, someone who squanders huge sums of money unnecessarily and without benefit, you have to be either really rich (however briefly) or a state – West Virginia for instance.

The New York Times recently published, "United States of Subsidies: a series examining business incentives and their impact on jobs and local economies", by Louise Story, Tiff Fehr, and Derek Watkins. The centerpiece of the series is a study that quantifies the amounts that states lavish on businesses in the form of incentives, subsidies, loans, grants, and other inducements ostensibly to generate commerce and create jobs.

Not surprisingly, the results of these inducements are frequently less than those predicted by the politicians and bureaucrats who promote them and the businesses that receive them. That may explain why West Virginia, a state with zero net job growth since the year 2000, is second among all states in per capita subsidies.

According to the Times study, West Virginia provides $1.57 billion – yes, that's "billion", not "million" – in subsidies and tax abatements to businesses every year. That's $845 for every man, woman, and child in the state. It's equivalent to 37% of the state's base budget and more than we allocate for education, or Medicaid, or roads, or prisons. In short, if business tax incentives were listed as an expenditure, it would be the state's single largest item in the budget.

By way of comparison, none of the states that border West Virginia spends even half as much. Pennsylvania is the next highest at $381 per person. As for the others, you have to add together Maryland ($96), Virginia ($161), Ohio ($281), and Kentucky ($324) in order to match West Virginia's generosity.

And West Virginia's use of tax incentives isn't necessitated because we start with unusually high tax rates. The Tax Foundation's 2013 ranking of state business tax climates rates West Virginia 23rd in the nation, ahead of all those neighboring states except for Pennsylvania, which comes in 19th.

So, what has our munificence won us, what has it cost us, and what does it mean?

As mentioned earlier, West Virginia has had no increase in the number of jobs in the state in the last 12 years. That's the period during which the state became most aggressive in cutting business taxes and extending incentives. While one can argue that conditions might have been worse in the absence of these measures, there's a stronger argument that the measures made little difference.

Peter Fisher, Research Director at the Iowa Policy Project, recently published an analysis showing state and local tax rates are not significant determinants of business growth. The reason is that these taxes make up a tiny fraction of business' operating costs. Business decisions about where to locate and whether or not to expand are far more influenced by factors such as demand for products and services, the availability of a qualified labor force, access to raw materials and suppliers, and infrastructure.

In fact, unless those needs are met first, the question of taxes doesn't even come into play. And, when it does, it's in the context of operating costs. In that area, West Virginia already offers wage and utility rates that are 20% below the national average – a market-based financial incentive that far outweighs any advantage to be offered through tax incentives.

Meanwhile, the loss of $1.57 billion a year in prospective business tax revenues has dire consequences for the rest of us. First, it's forcing West Virginia to make significant cuts to education and infrastructure at a time when, if we hope to attract and grow businesses, we must figure out ways to meet companies' needs for a skilled workforce, infrastructure, and an improved quality of life.

Second, West Virginia's tax burden is being shifted from businesses, many of which are out-of-state interests, to individual taxpayers. Since 2005, while the portion of state revenue collected from business income and franchise taxes has dropped from 13% to 4%, the portion collected from West Virginia families has risen from 30% to 42%.

And for what? Economic development? Or is it just corporate welfare? The problem is we can't tell the difference.

That's because, while handing out corporate goodies, West Virginia does almost nothing to track the results, either to hold companies accountable on those rare occasions when they actually make commitments to get the incentives, or merely to determine the state's return on investment.

In a way that's the worst aspect of the fiasco because, by itself, trying and failing to nurture business growth through tax incentives doesn't make our political leaders schmucks. It just means they've made mistakes. They become schmucks when, because they require no accountability, they don't know they've failed and, consequently, go on repeating the same mistake indefinitely or, in West Virginia's case, about 1.57 billion times per year. ■

EYES THAT DON'T LIE

December 22, 2012

Richard Pryor famously joked about a husband caught in bed with another woman by his wife. Rather than try to explain the inexplicable, the husband indignantly denies having an affair and even the existence of the woman beside him in bed.

"Who you gonna believe, me or your lying eyes?" he demands.

That is also the approximate reaction of West Virginia Commerce Secretary, Keith Burdette, to a recent New York Times story that shows West Virginia hands out $1.57 billion annually in tax exemptions, credits, and other subsidies to businesses with the ostensible goal of stimulating economic growth and jobs.

The result? West Virginia has had no net job growth in more than a decade.

The Times report, researched and written by Louise Story, is important because, if it's accurate, West Virginia gives away more than a third of its annual tax revenue even as the state cuts services for a population that is among the poorest, least educated, and least healthy in the nation.

That's probably why Secretary Burdette felt compelled to respond to the Times story. As reported by the Associated Press and Tom Miller in his "Under the Dome" column, Burdette told the Legislature's Joint Commission on Economic Development and the Joint Committee on Finance that the Times article was "poorly researched and reported" and presented a "woefully inadequate picture" of the state's use of tax incentives.

Burdette went on to say that the state issued only $83 million in tax credits last year and that $1.12 billion in sales tax exemptions shouldn't count as subsidies because the exemption is a standard piece of tax policy that exists in many states. The purpose is to avoid "double taxation" on intermediate goods and services that would otherwise be taxed again on sales to end-users. Moreover, Burdette argued, the $1.12 billion figure was exaggerated because the Times chose to report on a year, 2009, when power companies were making unusually large purchases of pollution control equipment. For these reasons, Burdette concluded, suggestions that West Virginia is second in the nation in the level of subsidies provided to business are misguided.

However, as impressive as Burdette's argument sounds, it's really nothing more than a complex if less funny variation on, "Who you gonna believe, me or your lying eyes?" Here's why.

First, Burdette didn't actually question the accuracy of the figures in the Times report. He was relegated to contextual objections because the Times supplemented its report with an online database that lists and quantifies each of the credits, grants, and other subsidies that comprise the $1.57 billion total.

To address the question of whether the $1.12 billion sales tax exemption counts as an incentive, I'll turn to another Sean O'Leary.

Sean O'Leary, the smarter, is a policy analyst at the West Virginia Center on Budget and Policy. In a recent blog post, he makes three points. First, the sales tax exemption, or "direct use exemption", applies only to specified businesses and industries, not all. Second, the state's 2010 Tax Expenditure Study explicitly says that, in addition to avoiding double taxation, the direct use exemption exists to "encourage investment in equipment and facilities by qualified industries." Finally, while most states have comparable policies, not all do.

In summary, O'Leary writes, "The direct use exemption meets all the definition(s) of a tax incentive: it is a tax preference for certain taxpayers engaged in certain activities, it is designed to encourage those activities, it saves businesses money compared to other states, and it deprives the state of a substantial amount of revenue."

O'Leary also addresses the question of whether the $1.12 billion in sales tax exemptions in 2009 was an aberration as Keith Burdette claimed. He writes, "The sales tax exemption is examined every three years, and the 2007 Tax Expenditure Study valued the direct use sales tax exemption at $1.1185 billion, with only a 4.9% increase from 2007 to 2010, which suggests that the 2010 figure was not excessively inflated."

In other words, The New York Times was right and, along with O'Leary, provides documentary evidence to prove it. West Virginia passes out $845 in business subsidies for every resident of the state and, if these incentives were listed as an expenditure in the state budget, they would constitute the single largest line item exceeding even education and healthcare.

Plus, there's another aspect of the story that has gone largely unaddressed – the state's unwillingness to share information about the business incentives it doles out and an associated absence of accountability.

In September the West Virginia Center on Budget and Policy prepared a presentation that concluded the state's "Tax Credit Review and Accountability Report" fails to provide data or analysis to determine if tax credits lead to additional jobs or economic impact, is only published every three years, includes only four business tax credits out of dozens of programs, and does not disclose the recipients of the credits.

Meanwhile, the New York Times database lists nineteen incentive programs for which the Commerce department refuses to make spending information available. That means the $1.57 billion figure is a floor rather than a ceiling on how much West Virginia metes out to businesses.

When asked to provide information about the missing nineteen programs and any information refuting data presented by the Times, Keith Burdette and the state Development Office chose not to respond.

Maybe they're afraid we'll believe our lying eyes. ∎

AN OUTBREAK OF INNUMERACY

October 30, 2012

It started on October 11th when Jared Hunt, a reporter for the Charleston Daily Mail, wrote an article that ran under the headline, "Md. casino vote could cost W.Va. $1 billion in revenue".

The projected loss, which would take place over ten years, is based on a study by the Sage Policy Group, a consulting firm commissioned by a political action committee that supports passage of Maryland's Question 7. The facility at risk of losing the revenue is West Virginia's Charles Town Hollywood Casino.

Hunt's article received considerable attention in West Virginia and was widely shared on Twitter. Hoppy Kercheval, host of West Virginia MetroNews Talkline, gave the report even greater notoriety when he invited Hunt to discuss the article on his statewide radio show.

Soon others were picking up on the story. Tom Miller, longtime writer of the "Under the Dome" column, which appears in numerous newspapers, devoted part of a column to the same study on which Hunt had reported. But, Miller's summary portrayed an even more horrific scenario.

Instead of a loss of $1 billion over ten years, Miller wrote that the loss would be as much as $1.5 billion. And more shocking, instead of taking place over ten years, Miller said the loss would be annual – an almost catastrophic outcome, since $1.5 billion represents 2% of the state's annual gross domestic product.

At this point, somebody's spidey-sense should have been tingling, indicating something was amiss. Not only is 2% of GDP a big number, but last year total revenue for Charles Town Hollywood Casino was only $570 million. How could the casino lose in revenue three times more than it takes in? But, concerns were allayed when Miller's column was promoted on Twitter by former West Virginia economics professor, Tom Witt.

With an endorsement like that, it just had to be true! Didn't it? Well, not really.

It turns out that the study upon which the reports were based does not say that West Virginia would lose $1.5 billion per year. It doesn't even say we would lose $1 billion over ten years.

The study projects that, in the event Maryland passes its referendum, Charles Town Hollywood Casino will lose $65 million dollars per year, which is fully one-third less than Jared Hunt reported and less than one-twentieth the amount Miller's column claimed.

Now, don't misunderstand, $65 million isn't chicken feed. It represents an 11% drop in revenue for Charles Town Hollywood Casino and might cost some jobs. But, it would not be catastrophic and would not by any stretch of the imagination put the casino's survival at risk as some readers of Hunt's and Miller's columns feared.

So the question is, how did prominent and respected people such as Hunt, Kercheval, Miller, and Witt get it wrong and, in Miller's and Witt's case, spectacularly wrong?

It's not as though the error had gone completely unnoticed. Bryan Clark, a reporter for The Spirit of Jefferson, a weekly newspaper in Jefferson County, which is home to Charles Town Hollywood Casino, noticed the mistake in Jared Hunt's original article and, in response, wrote a front-page story titled, "Reports of $1B casino loss wrong". His story appeared even before Miller's column.

Clark, who had read the study on which Hunt's original story was based and identified the mistake, was also aware that, before contradicting one of the state's leading newspapers, he had better be on solid ground. So, he did the logical thing. He called the study's author.

Anirban Basu, a principal at Sage Policy Group, confirmed that the projected loss to Charles Town Hollywood Casino would be between $60 million and $65 million per year. The $1.5 billion figure was mentioned in the report, but not as the amount Charles Town would lose if the referendum passes. $1.5 billion is the amount the study predicted Maryland residents would spend in Charles Town over a decade if the referendum is not passed.

However, under no circumstances would the creation of casinos in Maryland cause Charles Town to lose all of that business. Basu's team calculated that it would lose half or less, hence, the $60 million to $65 million per year figure.

There are many morals to this story having to do with the importance of thoroughness and attention to detail in reporting as well as the need for the public to practice critical reading skills. But, one lesson that should not be lost is the importance of quantitative literacy.

The error in Hunt's original story should have been suspected by anyone familiar with Charles Town Hollywood Casino's business. And the error made by Miller should have been obvious to anyone even vaguely familiar with the size of the state's economy.

Every day politicians, companies, organizations and their advocates hype stories that from a quantitative perspective and in the total scheme of things are nearly inconsequential – the imagined problem of pervasive voter fraud for instance. Meanwhile, other stories that are of great consequence, but in no one's interest to publicize, such as the $600 million windfall in annual federal subsidies that West Virginia would realize by fully expanding Medicaid to uninsured residents, receive little or no attention.

The sad part is that often the truth and weight of issues are right in front of us. But, because they're expressed numerically, we miss them altogether. ∎

ATTACK OF THE IDEOLOGUES

WEST VIRGINIA UNDER THE KNIFE

January 16, 2012

In December 2006 Curtis Dubay, Senior Economist for the Tax Foundation, delivered a briefing from the floor of the West Virginia House of Delegates in which he admired Ireland's Celtic Tiger economy and announced, "West Virginia should aim to be to the United States what Ireland is to Europe."

A year later the Irish real estate bubble burst and Ireland became the first of the anvils that still threaten to drag the European Union under. But, we shouldn't pick on Mr. Dubay because we were all insane that autumn.

In September of that year the Federal Reserve Board held a rollicking meeting at which Dallas Fed president Richard Fisher dismissed rumors of a housing bubble gleefully proclaiming, " the only subject that has been more analyzed than the housing situation is the birth of Brad Pitt's baby. (Laughter)".

The parenthetical "laughter" is in the actual transcript reminding us that we didn't just drive the economy off a cliff, but we did so with our foot on the accelerator and our eyes wide shut.

Ever since we've been trying to choose between two strategies for picking up the pieces – the Keynesian approach, championed by President Obama, which prescribes fiscal stimulus to reignite the economy, or the Austrian approach, championed by Republicans, which prescribes austerity and a reduction in the size of government.

So far Obama's strategy has generally held sway, but with major compromises forced on him when Republicans gained control of the House of Representatives in 2010. The result is a tepid recovery that pleases no one.

But, this election year gives us an opportunity to change as Republicans have realistic hopes of winning the presidency and the Senate while holding the House. Should that happen, something close to Wisconsin Congressman Paul Ryan's austerity-focused alternative federal budget, called the "Path to Prosperity", will probably be enacted. The question is, what would it mean for West Virginia?

On the spending side, the centerpiece of Ryan's plan is entitlement reform, which would change Medicare into a voucher program and reduce Medicaid. On the revenue side, Ryan would end the payroll tax cut and return those rates to previous levels while preserving the income tax cuts first enacted under President George W. Bush.

Before calculating the cost of these changes to West Virginia and to appreciate their significance, consider that a few weeks ago it was front-page news when the state announced $56 million in tax cuts for 2012. So, it's sobering to realize that, of the measures listed above, the one that would have the smallest impact – terminating the payroll tax cut – would take more than $500 million out of West Virginians' pockets – a loss almost ten times more than we saved with the state tax cut.

Cuts to Medicaid would cost West Virginia another $690 million annually. Finally, because changing Medicare to a voucher program would force recipients to pay market prices for medical care, beneficiaries would see an average cost increase of $6,250 annually. With more than 20% of West Virginians on Medicare, the cost to our state would be $2.4 billion.

The Ryan proposal contains other cuts as well, but these three items are sufficient to make a point. Taken together, they would remove more than $3.6 billion in discretionary income from West Virginians – more money than our entire coal industry pays in wages and severance taxes combined, $2,000 for every man, woman, and child in the state.

In short, it's huge and it would take immense economic growth to offset so large a hit. So, how much growth are places that have pursued government austerity achieving?

Back to Mr. Dubay's romantic Ireland. In the aftermath of the crash Ireland imposed huge government layoffs and pay cuts in a maniacal effort to reduce public debt and shrink government, hoping to reassure investors and spark growth. It hasn't happened.

Before the collapse, Ireland's unemployment rate like that of the US was about 4.5%. But, while our unemployment rate doubled before declining in recent months, Ireland's rate more than tripled. And rather than spike and fall like the US rate, Irish unemployment has stayed above 13% for two years and currently sits at 14.3%. Similarly, whereas American gross domestic demand (GDD) for goods and services returned to pre-crisis levels last year, Irish GDD has fallen for 14 consecutive quarters and the economy is expected to shrink further in 2012.

In fact, all of the countries where austerity policies have been implemented – Ireland, Greece, Spain, Italy, and Portugal – are listed among "The Economist" magazine's ten fastest shrinking economies of 2012.

In other words, the notion that cutting government will trigger economic expansion is at best a wish and, from all available evidence, not a likely one. What is certain and frightening are the reductions to West Virginia incomes and the increase in out-of pocket-costs that the Ryan budget would impose.

Nonetheless, when the Ryan budget was considered in congress last year, Representative Shelley Moore Capito voted "yea". On the other hand, first district congressman David McKinley was one of just four House Republicans voting against the bill and specifically cited its impact on Medicare as the reason.

Hopefully this year Capito and other members of our congressional delegation, including Senator Joe Manchin who is a wild card on this issue, will put dogma and political expediency aside long enough to look at the numbers, see the amount of money that an austerity budget would cost West Virginia, and realize the false promise and threat that austerity poses. ■

WALTER E. WILLIAMS' WAR WITH REALITY

April 29, 2012

Recently syndicated columnist Walter Williams noted that April 17th was Tax Day – the day until which we had to work this year to pay our combined federal, state, and local taxes.

Williams made this observation as preface to his argument that taxes are excessive and that federal budget deficits are strangling the economy. This position is also Republican Party dogma and is cited as justification for demanding tax and budget cuts.

Deficits, Williams explains, stifle economic growth because they result in government borrowing and inflation. Borrowing drives up interest rates leaving individuals and businesses with less to money to spend while inflation is "taxation by stealth" that debases the currency and takes yet more money out of our pockets.

Federal income taxes compound these problems by burdening the top 50% of earners with high marginal rates that they must endure because the other half of Americans pay little or nothing. Moreover, since non-payers have no stake in lowering tax rates, they support big-spending politicians and see tax cuts as a threat to the government's ability to give them "handouts".

It's a simple and compelling narrative – until it's compared to reality. So, let's do the comparison starting with Williams' criticism of the tax system.

Williams states "the top 1 percent of American income earners paid almost 37 percent of federal income taxes. The top 10 percent paid about 70 percent of federal income taxes, and the top 50 percent paid nearly 98 percent. Roughly 47 percent of Americans paid no federal income tax."

This sounds grotesquely unfair and would be, if federal income taxes were the only taxes we pay. But, when pointing out that it took us 107 days to reach Tax Day, Williams included all federal, state, and local taxes. So, when complaining about uneven distribution of taxes, why does he mention only the federal income tax?

Because, had Williams included all federal and state taxes, his claim that the burden is distributed unevenly would have been destroyed.

When all federal and state taxes are included, the top 1 percent of taxpayers, who earn an average of $1.4 million annually, shoulders just 21.6 percent of the burden matching almost exactly their share of the nation's total income – 21 percent.

Additionally, the top 1 percent's total combined tax rate of 29 percent is almost the same as that of families making $68,000 per year whose combined rate is 28.3 percent. The only people who pay less than 20 percent of their income in taxes are the lowest earners whose average income is $13,000 per year. They pay 17.4%.

In short, the higher federal income tax rates experienced by the wealthy are almost entirely offset by Social Security and state taxes which exact a much larger share of incomes from middle and lower income earners.

As a side note, Williams' accompanying surmise that "people who pay little or no taxes become constituents for big-spending politicians", seems odd when most o f the income-poor states, including West Virginia, that pay comparatively little in income taxes and depend heavily on federal "handouts" voted decisively for the Republican presidential candidate in the last election.

But, what about Williams' implication that deficits and inflation suffocate the economy?

In the late 1990's the federal government ran budget surpluses. Then came the income tax cuts passed under President George W. Bush and increases in military spending for wars in Iraq and Afghanistan. Large deficits ensued and the national debt grew by more than half. Then came the housing bubble and the economy crashed in 2007 and 2008. Tax revenues plunged and deficits became even greater as more people required assistance from safety-net programs.

It was exactly the high borrowing, deficit spending doomsday scenario Williams described and, if his theory were correct, the result by now should have been years of high interest rates and rampant inflation. But, both continue to be at lows not seen in fifty years.

Meanwhile, Williams' other predicted result, slow economic growth, is contradicted by history. In 1947, after years of deficit spending during World War II and continued deficit spending on the GI Bill and other programs, the national debt reached an all-time high as a percent of GDP – even larger than today's debt. Yet, we didn't cut budgets and impose austerity measures. And the result wasn't economic ruin. It was the longest and most robust economic expansion in history during which deficits shrank and the debt declined as a percent of GDP.

We could have the same result today if Williams' Republican co-religionists in congress would support rather than fight stimulus measures. Economic text books have long taught that, instead of hewing to the dogma of always balanced budgets, deficit spending can and should be used to stimulate the economy in times of slowdown and surpluses should be run in times of growth. The wisdom of that approach was proven in the bountiful decades that followed World War II and the price of ignoring that wisdom is evident in the now years-long economic downturn of European countries that made the mistake of actually applying Williams' preferred policies.

In summary, Williams' fears are repudiated by our historically low interest and inflation rates and by the post-World War II boom. And his belief in the virtues of austerity is repudiated by what has become a European depression. The question is whether Williams and Republicans in congress will finally give reality its due. ∎

WEST VIRGINIA AND THE TAX CUT FAIRY

May 23, 2012

Some people believe Senator Joe Manchin will run for president someday. If he does, Manchin will almost certainly tout his term as West Virginia governor during which he cut taxes and balanced budgets in one of the most economically depressed states in the union. And, if Manchin's candidacy gains traction, his opponents will respond.

They'll say, "Joe, anyone can balance a budget if you're willing to settle for the worst schools, the worst healthcare, and the worst infrastructure in the nation. West Virginia is the poorest, least educated, and unhealthiest state in America. Is that what we want for the country?"

The accusation won't be entirely fair. West Virginia isn't the worst state in every category. In some, we rank as high as 47th or 48th. But, for political purposes, the claim will be true enough. West Virginians will be humiliated and Manchin's candidacy will come to an ignominious end.

This gaze into the future isn't done to help Joe Manchin with his career choices. It's to point out that as governor Manchin aggressively cut business taxes in order to grow West Virginia's moribund economy and it didn't work. The price we're now paying isn't just the lowest level of adult employment in the country, but also chronic under-investment in the state and its people, which means our future prospects are as dim as our present situation. And worse, current governor Earl Ray Tomblin and the legislature continue to pursue the same failed policies.

But, why did the strategy fail? And why do we continue to believe in the tax cut fairy?

Basically there have been two kinds of tax cuts: reductions in the Corporate Net Income and Business Franchise taxes (CNIT/BFT), which apply to all businesses, and targeted tax incentives, such as those offered to Shell Oil in our failed pursuit of the ethane cracker plant. Examining both types requires more space than a single column permits. So, today we'll focus on CNIT/BFT and in two weeks explore targeted tax incentives.

The theory behind cutting CNIT/BFT is that it puts money in the pockets of businesses enabling them to expand and hire more people, while making West Virginia more competitive with other states in attracting new businesses.

As Ted Boettner and the West Virginia Center on Budget and Policy has thoroughly documented, CNIT/BFT, which made up almost 13 percent of general fund revenues in 1990, has been cut to the point that they comprise only about 4 percent in 2012, forcing personal income taxes and severance taxes to make up for the loss. Additionally, CNIT/BFT is scheduled for further cuts over the next three years and businesses are now lobbying for cuts to the state's Business Personal Property Tax as well.

Yet there has been little or no incremental growth and the state's ability to address education, infrastructure, and healthcare issues has been hobbled.

The reason is that, while in the right conditions business tax cuts can be effective, those conditions don't exist in West Virginia and aren't likely to anytime soon.

Business tax cuts work when businesses want to expand, but can't because funding through loans and other instruments is prohibitively expensive. Today, however, we have precisely the opposite situation. Interest rates have never been lower making funding inexpensive even without tax cuts.

Moreover, cheap money or not, businesses don't expand and hire unless they must to meet demand for their products. But, we're still feeling the effects of a recession whose signature characteristic was a drying up of demand, which from all indications will continue to be weak.

Third, as a percent of business's operating costs, the tax cuts are so small and spread so thin, they're not sufficient to change business behavior and end up rewarding businesses for doing what they would have done anyway.

Fourth, West Virginia's business tax environment is already quite competitive ranking 23rd among all states in the Tax Foundation's latest State Business Tax Climate Index.

Finally, much of the money that companies receive from tax cuts leaves the state. West Virginia is unusually dependent on out-of-state employers. When Wal-Mart, the state's largest employer, gets a tax cut, the savings go to corporate headquarters in Arkansas.

The result is that money is squandered with little gain. So, why in the absence of beneficial results, do our leaders continue to believe in the tax cut fairy? Probably because cutting taxes can be dressed up as good public policy and it pleases important constituents.

But, in the absence of the right conditions, we only manage to cripple the state's ability to address the fundamental issues that discourage businesses from locating and expanding in West Virginia – the lack of an educated workforce, inadequate infrastructure, and a poor quality of life.

By choosing to hand out ineffectual tax cuts rather than address these issues more aggressively, the governor and legislature are basically conceding that they lack ideas, motivation, and the expectation that the challenges can be overcome.

Some will object that West Virginia is, in fact, working hard to address these problems and that in some areas the state's effort is equal to or greater than national averages. But, to use a medical analogy, some states have an economic cold and others have the flu, but West Virginia has cancer and cancer requires more than an average level of treatment.

In two weeks, we'll peer into the state's intentionally murky efforts to lure businesses and jobs to West Virginia with targeted tax incentives. ■

WEST VIRGINIA AND THE TAX-CUT FAIRY — PART II

June 10, 2012

This month Century Aluminum petitioned the West Virginia Public Utility Commission for a special rate for the purchase of electricity as part of its joint effort with the state to reopen a Ravenswood plant that closed in 2009 resulting in 650 workers being laid off.

But a third party response to Century's petition warns that the cost of the requested subsidy is "staggeringly high". While reminding the PUC that the goal is "a thriving Ravenswood plant, competitive over the long term", the response explains why that outcome isn't likely. It suggests that Century may board up the plant when the subsidy ends in 2021 noting that the company's own appraisers reported in 2009 that the plant "suffers from severe functional and technological obsolescence". Nor is there any indication that Century intends to invest in modernization.

But the response's most scathing criticism is that the rate request will result in a "guaranteed profit margin" for Century, insulating it from business risk and passing costs to West Virginia rate-payers, perhaps adding as much as $144 annually to the average residential electric bill. When combined with additional tax incentives already passed by the state legislature, the total taxpayer-funded subsidy comes to between $40 and $50 million dollars a year.

This is the kind of indictment you would expect from a do-gooder public interest group. Except that's not where it came from.

The response was submitted by Appalachian Power Company, the electric company that stands to see its business grow by about 10% in West Virginia if the PUC approves Century's petition. So, why is APCo, an apparent beneficiary, raising concerns? And why in the face of these issues did the legislature approve its part of the deal with almost no debate and only one dissenting vote?

The answers to these questions speak volumes about the doubtful math, craven politics, and absence of accountability surrounding targeted tax incentives which can cost hundreds of millions of dollars and whose results are almost never analyzed.

In recent months, in addition to the Century incentives, the state offered $84 million worth of incentives to Gestamp, a German auto parts manufacturer, for the location of a plant in South Charleston and over $300 million to Royal Dutch Shell for the famous ethane cracker plant that was lost to Pennsylvania.

Why is the state so generous? "Jobs", we are told – about 400 associated with both the Century and Gestamp deals and as many as 20,000 associated with the Shell cracker plant according to the governor. But, the question is, at what cost?

A common denominator of the Century and Shell incentive packages is that the administration claims there would be zero cost to the state since the incentives apply only to hypothetical future revenues and have no effect on current income. Of course, this argument blithely ignores the Century deal's possible hike in electric rates, which isn't counted as a cost to the state because the proceeds would go directly to APCo.

As for additional costs stemming from increased demand for public services – schools, roads, police, the courts, etc. – the administration insists these would be offset by increased income taxes collected from newly employed workers. But, the math behind such claims is unverifiable because the state refuses to reveal its underlying assumptions.

This refusal is assisted by a provision in state law that exempts many West Virginia Development Office documents from Freedom of Information requirements. And in a state where politicians and industries regularly overstate benefits and understate costs, there's little reason to have confidence in the administration's claims, particularly when there is valuable political capital to be gained by "creating jobs".

A second problem is that, while some targeted incentives are designed to help West Virginia compete with other states, as in the case of the cracker plant, others merely subsidize ventures that the free market has determined are economically non-viable. That's the case with Century.

In addition to concerns about obsolescence at the Ravenswood plant, Century's financial condition is uncertain. Since 2008 Century's stock price has dropped by 90 percent from a high of $75 a share to just over $7 a share. The investment management firm Macroaxis puts Century's chances of going bankrupt at 43 percent.

Moreover, Century's subsidies are pegged to the market price of aluminum to insure that the company makes a profit. The lower aluminum prices go and the worse Century's business environment becomes, the more money West Virginia taxpayers must fork over. It's "heads, Century wins and tails, West Virginia taxpayers lose".

Finally, targeted tax incentives have a corrosive effect on the state's ability to raise revenue. When one company gets a special break, resistance to new taxes from other taxpayers and pressure for compensatory tax relief increases, making it more difficult for the state to fund vital services. A similar consideration almost certainly contributed to APCo's concerns about the Century deal. If APCo customers have to absorb rate increases because of Century, they and the PUC will be less receptive to future rate increase requests that APCo may request for its own purposes.

These are the kinds of dynamics that make targeted tax incentives abhorrent not just to left-leaning public interest groups, but also to conservative ones such as the Tax Foundation. And their concerns are especially pertinent in a state such as West Virginia that shrouds its economic assumptions in secrecy and practices little accountability once incentives are given. ■

THE WEST VIRGINIA PROTECTION PLEDGE

July 14, 2012

Political pledges are usually pernicious. They tie office-holders to policy prescriptions long after time and circumstances render them irrelevant or harmful. They inhibit compromise, which is, though some won't admit it, the oil that prevents the engines of government and society from seizing up. And it was Edmund Burke who cautioned us that pledges represent an abdication of judgment and responsibility.

Still, congresswoman Shelley Moore Capito of West Virginia's second district and David McKinley of the first, signed Grover Norquist's well-known Taxpayer Protection Pledge, which obligates signatories to oppose any increase in marginal income tax rates and to offset any elimination of deductions with corresponding cuts in rates.

Rather than debate the doubtful merits of the pledge, let's accept it as accomplished fact and consider that it may need to be counterbalanced with another pledge whose benefits are more certain. It reads:

"I will oppose any budget and tax package that takes more from West Virginia in budget cuts than it returns in tax cuts."

Call it the West Virginia Protection Pledge. It simply says that state taxpayers must get back at least as much money in tax cuts as we sacrifice in budget cuts so that we're not made poorer than we already are. This shouldn't be a difficult commitment for representatives who are, after all, elected to represent our interests.

But, for Capito and McKinley, it will be difficult because it's probably mathematically impossible to adhere to both a West Virginia Protection Pledge and to Norquist's pledge. It's also unlikely that they can honor the West Virginia Protection pledge while supporting the budget and tax plans proposed by presidential candidate, Mitt Romney, and Republican congressman Paul Ryan.

Here's why.

According to the Tax Policy Center of the Brookings Institution and the Urban Institute, 95% of the tax cut savings proposed in Romney's plan would go to households with incomes of more than $100,000 a year and 70% would go to those making more than $200,000.

But, in West Virginia we don't have very many people in either category. While nationally more than a quarter of households make over $100,000 a year, in West Virginia only 11% do. And, while more than 5% of US households make more than $200,000, in West Virginia the number is just over 1%.

In all, we have only a third as many wealthy people as the nation and twice as many poor people. And, under the Romney plan, taxes for many middle class and poorer people will, if anything, go up due to the elimination of some tax deductions.

This will produce a result similar to what happened with the Bush tax cuts of a decade ago when West Virginians received only 67 cents in savings for every dollar received by other Americans. Except this time will be worse because the Romney and Ryan cuts are more skewed to benefit the wealthy than the Bush tax cuts were. In fact, because both the Romney and Ryan plans involve removing deductions, most West Virginians will probably see an income tax increase.

Then there are the looming cuts to entitlements. West Virginia receives more than twice as many dollars in federal spending as we contribute in taxes. Much of that spending comes from programs Republicans are targeting for cuts such as disability, Medicare, Medicaid, and food stamps. So, to the degree these programs are reduced, West Virginia will suffer disproportionately probably leaving the state in a "net loss" situation in which more money is removed from the state's economy than is put back in.

The consequent reductions in personal income and in retail demand could be profound for West Virginia citizens and merchants producing precisely the opposite result of the one which Republicans intend, which is to put more not less money in Americans' pockets.

It's reasonable to question the wisdom of a policy that would punish one of the nation's poorest states so. Perhaps the policy could be justified if, despite the damage to West Virginia, it benefitted the nation as a whole. Unfortunately, the evidence suggests otherwise.

As Nobel Prize-winning economist, Joseph Stiglitz, said recently in an interview with Rolling Stone Magazine, "No large economy has ever recovered from an economic downturn through austerity." He was referring specifically to the Republican strategy of slashing government spending, which, not coincidentally, is being practiced with stunningly awful results in European countries such as Ireland and Spain.

West Virginia wouldn't be the only state to face a net loss catastrophe. But, we would be the first and the most seriously damaged while the nation as a whole would suffer as well.

The principles on which Republicans base their policies sound wise – Tax cuts are good, budgets should be balanced, and social programs shouldn't breed dependency. But, the road to hell, as they say, is paved with good intentions. Besides, the marketplace isn't based on the exchange of principles. It's based on the exchange of money and when the Romney and Ryan plans are monetized, West Virginia and America end up losers.

It's too much to say that what's good for West Virginia is good for the country, but it's not too much to say that what's bad for West Virginia is bad for the country. So, the question stands.

When push comes to shove, which pledge will our congressional representatives honor, the West Virginia Protection pledge and with it the national interest, or the Grover Norquist pledge and party ideology? ∎

GIVING IDEOLOGY A HOLIDAY

June 4, 2010

In "Civil Disobedience" Henry David Thoreau gave us some of the most frequently quoted lines in political discourse.

He wrote, "That government is best which governs least" and, rethinking the point, modified it to say, "That government is best which governs not at all and when men are prepared for it, that will be the kind of government which they will have."

These lines are favorites because there's something for everyone. Republicans and Libertarians love "That government is best which governs least". Anarchists adore "That government is best which governs not at all". And liberals see the wry, "and when men are prepared for it, that will be the kind of government which they will have" as a reminder that minimal government is not the means to a good society, but rather an end which is only produced after men become so virtuous they no longer need law and governance, a situation we haven't yet attained.

Thoreau probably thought he was enunciating a single, coherent principle and would be astonished at the range of ideologies that make use of his words; a reminder of how malleable principles can be and how lazy ideology can make us.

Ideologues, whether Marxists, Christians, Libertarians, or Socialists, feeling possessed of one big truth often disregard smaller truths – those of history, economics, biology, and physics for instance. Libertarian and Republican Senate candidate Rand Paul of Kentucky recently demonstrated breathtaking unconcern for two centuries of racial strife when he blithely dismissed the need for civil rights laws based on his dogmatic belief that free markets inevitably wring parochialisms such as racism from commerce and, therefore, from our souls – history be damned.

So, if mutable principles and ideological myopia can produce such silliness, maybe they also explain why people sometimes support policies that history and economics suggest would not only be disastrous, but would harm them most of all.

I'm speaking of positions promoted on the web site of We The People of Jefferson County, a local Tea Party affiliate.

Take as an example opposition to healthcare reform. The Tea Party's stand for the elimination of wasteful spending makes its defense of our traditional healthcare system quite mysterious because, whether measured by cost or outcomes, the US system has been the most expensive and least effective of any in the industrialized world.

In 2007 we spent $7,290 per person for healthcare, twice that of "socialized medicine" punching bags Canada, the United Kingdom, France, and Germany. Yet, those countries enjoy longer life spans and lower infant mortality than we do. Plus, they cover everyone.

If we were as efficient, the US would save a trillion dollars annually – enough to eliminate all budget deficits. Plus, we'd live longer. To rage against virtually any role for the federal government in healthcare can only be classified as a case of ideology trumping performance and it amounts to a defense of our right to be gouged.

Tea Party opposition to government regulation has a similarly self-destructive quality. The litany of recent disasters attributable to insufficient or non-existent government regulation is staggering. Since the 1980's, the dawn of the privatization and deregulation era, we've endured successive fiascos starting with the Savings and Loan crisis, followed by Enron, and culminating in the housing market meltdown, which precipitated the near collapse of the financial system. In every case the losers have principally been the middle class.

Contrary to the dogma of free market purists, experience demonstrates that markets, while useful, are neither flawless nor self-correcting. You don't have to be a socialist to recognize that markets are a tool to be used, not a god to be worshipped and that effective government regulation is an aide, not a barrier, to stability and prosperity.

Then, there are taxes about which the We The People web site uses terms such as tyrannical, confiscatory and redistributive. In fact, tax rates on the highest earners are at their lowest rate since 1931 except for a brief period from 1988 to 1992. And, those who campaign for elimination of Estate and Capital Gains taxes, must be unaware that these taxes have little or no impact on middle class Americans and that elimination can only result in increased budget deficits and/or increases in other taxes that are paid by the middle class.

Of course, that would just continue a pattern of wealth redistribution that, for the past two decades, has gone not from rich to poor, but from the poor and middle class to the rich. And, haven't the results been great? Middle class families have been working harder for years for little or no increase in wealth and standard of living ...and now the bottom has fallen out.

Under the circumstances it's not surprising that many in the middle class, not just Tea Partiers, resent bailouts of banks and automobile companies and worry about increasing deficits. So, perhaps we can set ideology aside and consider the notion that best the way to prevent bailouts is to impose effective regulation that prevents individual commercial entities from becoming so large that their failure threatens the entire economy. And, while working to eliminate wasteful spending, a point on which we can all agree, let's also consider that the last president to try to balance the federal budget during a recession was Herbert Hoover – and we got the Great Depression. ∎

STATESMEN AND OTHERS

AN EXAMINED LIFE

July 5, 2010

Robert Byrd was born into a world of hard-edged racism, anti-intellectualism, and the fundamentalist penchant for seeing doubt as weakness and compromise as surrender. To this he added a bounding ambition and emerged an utterly assured, reflexively hawkish politician for whom hubris might have been just a water-stop on the way to megalomania.

But, fate intervened. While pursuing an education he hoped would make him more electable, Byrd, perhaps inadvertently, paid attention to what was being taught. So, on March 19, 2003 an older and different Byrd, seasoned by decades of experience and animated by an astonishing commitment to unflinching self-examination, spoke these words in the United States Senate as the nation plunged toward war in Iraq.

"I believe in this beautiful country. I have studied its roots and gloried in the wisdom of its magnificent Constitution. I have marveled at the wisdom of its founders and framers. Generation after generation of Americans has understood the lofty ideals that underlie our great Republic. I have been inspired by the story of their sacrifice and their strength. But, today I weep for my country. I have watched the events of recent months with a heavy, heavy heart. No more is the image of America one of strong, yet benevolent peacekeeper. The image of America has changed. Around the globe, our friends mistrust us, our word is disputed, our intentions are questioned.'

'Instead of reasoning with those with whom we disagree, we demand obedience or threaten recrimination. Instead of isolating Saddam Hussein, we seem to have isolated ourselves. We proclaim a new doctrine of preemption, which is understood by few and feared by many. We say that the United States has the right to turn its firepower on any corner of the globe, which might be suspect in the war on terrorism. We assert that right without the sanction of any international body. As a result, the world has become a much more dangerous place.'

'We flaunt our superpower status with arrogance. We treat UN Security Council members like ingrates who offend our princely dignity by lifting their heads from the carpet. Valuable alliances are split.'

'After war has ended, the United States will have to rebuild much more than the country of Iraq. We will have to rebuild America's image around the globe.'

'The case this Administration tries to make to justify its fixation with war is tainted by charges of falsified documents and circumstantial evidence. We cannot convince the world of the necessity of this war for one simple reason. This is a war of choice.'

'There is no credible information to connect Saddam Hussein to 9/11. The twin towers fell because a world-wide terrorist group, Al Qaeda ....'

'The brutality seen on September 11th and in other terrorist attacks we have witnessed around the globe are the violent and desperate efforts by extremists to stop the daily encroachment of western values upon their cultures. That is what we fight... .'

'But, this Administration has directed all of the anger, fear, and grief which emerged from the ashes of the twin towers and the twisted metal of the Pentagon towards a tangible villain, one we can see and hate and attack. And villain he is. But, he is the wrong villain. And this is the wrong war...'

'There is a pervasive sense of rush and risk and too many questions unanswered. How long will we be in Iraq? What will be the cost? What is the ultimate mission? How great is the danger at home?'

'A pall has fallen over the Senate Chamber. We avoid our solemn duty to debate the one topic on the minds of all Americans, even while scores of thousands of our sons and daughters faithfully do their duty in Iraq.'

'What is happening to this country? When did we become a nation which ignores and berates our friends? When did we decide to risk undermining international order by adopting a radical and doctrinaire approach to using our awesome military might? How can we abandon diplomatic efforts when the turmoil in the world cries out for diplomacy?'

'Why can this President not seem to see that America's true power lies not in its will to intimidate, but in its ability to inspire?'

'War appears inevitable. But, I continue to hope that the cloud will lift. Saddam will yet turn tail and run. Perhaps reason will somehow still prevail. I along with millions of Americans will pray for the safety of our troops, for the innocent civilians in Iraq, and for the security of our homeland. May God continue to bless the United States of America in the troubled days ahead, and may we somehow recapture the vision which for the present eludes us."

He counseled humility when we would brook no doubt, dissent when we demanded conformity and restraint when we craved the cathartic orgy of "shock and awe". And in every particular Senator Byrd was proven right and the President, the Vice President, 97 senators, and the majority of Americans were proven wrong.

He was courageous, prescient, and articulated American values even as they evaporated. His words will forever belie the excuse that "everyone believed Saddam Hussein had weapons of mass destruction" and will stand as a monument to self-examination and those with the courage to practice it. ■

SENATOR BYRD EXPLAINS IT ALL

October 3, 2012

When I returned home from last Tuesday's debate between United States senate candidates Joe Manchin and John Raese, my phone was ringing.

ME: Hello.

CALLER: Sean, do you know who this is?

ME: Senator Byrd? But, how …?

CALLER: It's the new direct line back to West Virginia. When I got here, they had an opening on the appropriations committee and this is my first earmark.

ME: There's an appropriations committee in …?

CALLER: Never mind about that. Are you planning to write a column about tonight's debate?

ME: Sure. Do you have any thoughts?

CALLER: As a matter of fact, I do.

ME: Shoot.

CALLER: I'm troubled because we seem to have lost our memory, our ability to learn from the past. Both candidates talk about the current economic crisis as though it's unprecedented. But, there's nothing new about high unemployment and a large national debt. In the 1930's, unemployment was three times what it is now and by 1950 the national debt was every bit as great.

ME: But, isn't that why both Manchin and Raese want to cut taxes and cap spending?

CALLER: Of course. But, will it work? What evidence is there that cutting taxes for the wealthy and gutting social programs will get this economy going again? None! Taxes on the wealthy are already at their lowest point in 70 years. Has it worked? Under Presidents Eisenhower, and Kennedy top income tax rates were twice what they are now and our economy boomed. And arbitrarily capping spending simply limits our ability to respond to crises – wars and economic downturns.

ME: But, if we don't shrink government, how will we pay down the debt?

CALLER: How did we get rid of our debt in the 1950's and 1960's? We grew our way out. We invested in dams, highways, and airports. Jobs were created. And that created demand for private sector goods and services. The economy grew and generated tax receipts that reduced the debt. Without growth, no amount of cutting can balance the budget. Look at Europe where they're trying to cut their way to prosperity. Unemployment is higher than ever and their economies are still shrinking.

ME: But, won't Social Security and entitlements sink us?

CALLER: For sixty years we raided Social Security surpluses to pay for the rest of government including wars in Vietnam, Iraq, and Afghanistan. If we hadn't raided Social Security, its finances would be in fine shape today and for another sixty years. So, to complain that Social Security is the cause of the debt is pure demagoguery.

ME: What about other entitlements?

CALLER: You're talking about programs that help the poor, the unemployed, and students. Let me tell you something. During the Great Depression, before child nutrition and unemployment insurance, people starved in this country. Life expectancy actually declined because people couldn't find work and enough to eat. How do we expect people to pull themselves out of poverty if they can't get food and an education?

ME: What about Obamacare? Raese wants to repeal it and Manchin says it needs to be modified.

CALLER: The problem with Joe's position is that the parts he wants to modify are needed to pay for the parts he wants to keep. The problem with outright repeal is that it throws us back into the situation we had before. 50 million Americans uninsured and the highest healthcare costs in the world. Great Britain, France, Germany, Canada, and other countries all have healthcare systems that take better care of their people at half the cost. Half! Is Obamacare perfect? No. But, it's a step in the right direction and it helps West Virginia more than any other state.

ME: What did you think of Manchin and Raese both insisting the EPA is conducting a war on coal?

CALLER: I grieve when I hear Joe and Raese harping on the EPA. It's a distraction conjured up by the industry, which continues to stick its head in the sand. We could abolish the EPA tomorrow and coal wouldn't make a comeback because natural gas is cheaper, cleaner, and more plentiful and will continue to be for decades.

But, there's something else that grieves me more. In all the talk about the coal industry neither candidate mentioned our miners and what's happening to them. Black lung disease is back to the levels it was at in the 1970's and thousands of retired miners may lose their pensions because Patriot Coal Company is using a New York bankruptcy court to try to avoid its legal obligation to pay these men and their families. It's shameful that both men ignore it.

ME: You don't sound very pleased about either candidate taking your old senate seat.

CALLER: It's not my seat and it won't be Joe's seat or Raese's seat either. It belongs to the people of West Virginia. You remind them, that's who they serve – not their political parties and not the moneyed interests that try to dress up private agendas as good public policy.

ME: I'll do that.

CALLER: And, when you see Joe, tell him I wish he'd return my calls.

ME: I will, Senator. It's good to hear from you again.

CALLER: I'm glad somebody thinks so. But, now it's late and we both should get some sleep. Good night.

ME: Night, Senator. And take care up there. ∎

THE END OF JAY, THE END OF AN ERA

January 13, 2013

It's a problem as old as elections. Newly chosen representatives ask themselves, "Should my actions be guided by the will of the majority of my constituents or by my own judgment?"

Some resolve to always follow their constituents' wishes. But eventually, as they are inundated by facts and considerations too arcane or sensitive to enter public discourse, as they confront witheringly complex bills containing multiple provisions some of which are popular and some not, and as they contemplate their duty to represent all of their constituents including those in the minority, representatives eventually find the exercise of personal judgment unavoidable. Initially they may do so in lieu of guidance from their constituents, but inevitably, in some instances, they do so in opposition to it.

That's how it was meant to be. The Constitution places many buffers between the popular will and the enactment of laws. Legislators, especially senators, are encouraged to exercise judgment by provisions that insulate them from the whims of public opinion.

Still, even in a system that encourages legislative independence, the degree to which it was exercised by West Virginia's former senator Robert Byrd and by its current, but soon-to-retire senator, Jay Rockefeller, is remarkable. Equally remarkable is that two men from opposite ends of any economic, social, or cultural scale one can imagine should end so near to one another in how they perceive West Virginia, the nation, and the forces that shape us.

For decades Byrd and Rockefeller were to the left of their electorate on issues ranging from fiscal policy and social issues to the environment and, of course, coal. On issue after issue, had referenda been held, West Virginia's voters would have come down on the side opposite that of their senators.

That's not to say Byrd and Rockefeller always acted in opposition to the preferences of their constituents. But, while they did what they thought best and many West Virginians agreed with them, on some important issues more probably did not.

Still, voters elected and re-elected them – Byrd nine times and Rockefeller six. But why, when so often they went against our collective wishes?

To say it was "habit" is to duck the question. And, while it's true that their election opponents were often tomato cans, that too is an evasion. There was something more subtle and important.

Byrd and Rockefeller won elections because, for reasons going back to their origins, they commanded not just our trust, but our deference – our willingness to place greater faith in their judgment than we place in our own.

In Byrd's case, it's because he was one of us and his love of West Virginia was palpable. So, we willingly accompanied him in his personal evolution from Dixiecrat segregationist to defender of the Constitution and conscience of the Senate.

Rockefeller on the other hand has never been one of us. How could he be? He came along at a time when Governor Arch Moore, who was one of us, was revealing the ugliness and folly of our tendency to put the state on the block to the highest bidder – usually the coal industry.

But, it was also a time when we weren't so cowed by corporate fear mongering and threats of job loss. So, as Arch Moore slouched from office, doing a few last favors for his cronies before being convicted of extortion, we elected an outsider, Rockefeller, to replace him, in no small part because we had seen where placing trust in the coal industry and its apologists led.

Far from being a "carpetbagger" as some charged, Rockefeller proved to be deeply committed to West Virginia. In contrast to his predecessor, he could be trusted to act in what he believed to be the best interest of West Virginians.

In the senate, Byrd became and Rockefeller always was more liberal than most West Virginians, which caused some to call our willingness to elect and re-elect them an abdication of responsibility by voters. But, it was no more an abdication than when we defer to doctors, financial advisors, and other experts in matters in which we reasonably believe that their choices, while sometimes mysterious to us, are guided by superior knowledge and judgment.

Meanwhile, Byrd and Rockefeller rarely needed or sought constituent approval, which was OK, because they usually chose well. But, it also left a void.

Feeling little need to persuade constituents of the virtues of their policies, Byrd and Rockefeller participated less and less in West Virginia's political discourse, ceding that role to a succession of governors who have become progressively more conservative, who tied our economic prospects to a fading coal industry that never made West Virginia prosperous, and who, despite all evidence to the contrary, accept at face value the fiction that cutting business taxes and public safety even a the cost of reducing investment in the state and its people will somehow produce economic prosperity. It's a creed that today few leaders in West Virginia question much less challenge.

So, as Jay Rockefeller's resignation represents an end to our era of patrician senators, we will, for the first time in generations, be guided by our own lights rather than by theirs. New senators will be chosen based on the degree to which their beliefs coincide with our own. But, what should we believe?

If only as a final act of deference, we should study and contemplate why Senators Byrd and Rockefeller believed differently than we do on so many issues, including economic policy, coal, and healthcare, and only then decide which set of beliefs would best serve West Virginia and the nation and should be our standard when considering who we want to represent us and how. ■

THE HOBGOBLINS OF JOE MANCHIN

December 12, 2011

If this was the Comedy Central's "The Daily Show", you would now see a video of Senator Joe Manchin discoursing on the folly of ending tax cuts in time of economic distress. He would assure us that deficits produced by tax cuts can easily be offset by eliminating government waste. And he would seal his sermon by reminding us that he will "do anything to put more money in the pockets of West Virginians".

Then Jon Stewart would appear confidently saying, "So, Senator Manchin's vote on the payroll tax cut is entirely predictable", whereupon we would cut back to Manchin who would continue with, "…therefore, I do not support an extension of the payroll tax cut because this nation cannot afford another dime of debt. There's no evidence this tax cut creates jobs and it only puts $14.50 a week in the pockets of taxpayers. Most people probably don't know they're getting it."

Flash back to John Stewart and see his famous look of bafflement as he struggles to reconcile Manchin's turnabout – all the reasons the Senator gave for supporting tax cuts suddenly turned upside down because …because …? Well, it's hard to figure out really.

In fairness to Senator Manchin, the preceding statements were made at different times and were in fact pieced together from comments he made about two entirely different tax bills.

The first segment, supporting tax cuts, was assembled from claims he made prior to voting to extend income tax cuts originally enacted under President George W. Bush. At that time Manchin bucked his party and President Obama who charged that the Bush cuts added to the federal deficit, did little to create jobs, and disproportionately favored the rich.

The second segment, opposing tax cuts, came from remarks Manchin made last week when voting against an extension of the payroll tax cut originally enacted earlier this year under President Obama.

Given his contradictory arguments, we could wonder why Manchin would support one tax cut, but not the other. But, the better question is, if he was going to support only one, why would it be the Bush tax cuts since the well-being of West Virginia and of the country would seem to dictate the reverse as a simple comparison shows.

West Virginia is a great place to compare extensions of the two tax cuts because both return about the same amount of money, $750 million annually, to West Virginians. But, beyond that, their effects are quite different.

Under the Bush tax cuts, West Virginia fares poorly. Because the wealthy are favored and West Virginians have the lowest incomes in the nation, we receive only about sixty-seven cents in savings for every dollar that other Americans receive, also putting us last in the nation. Meanwhile, the Bush tax cuts add $330 billion annually to the federal deficit and, although they have been in place for nearly a decade, they show little evidence of generating jobs or growth.

The payroll tax cut, on the other hand, delivers the same total savings for West Virginians and does so at rate that's much closer to parity with the rest of the nation. It adds only $182 billion to the deficit and the benefits are more broadly shared among West Virginia households than those of the Bush tax cut. The payroll tax cut hasn't been around long enough to determine its effects on the economy or jobs, but a 2010 Congressional Budget Office analysis predicted that, all things being equal, the payroll tax cut has four times the job growth impact of the Bush tax cuts.

In short, whether you agree with the arguments Joe Manchin made in support of tax cut extensions or opposing them, the payroll tax cut seems the better option for West Virginia and the nation. Yet, his votes were exactly the reverse. Why?

It's an important question because ending the payroll tax cut constitutes a major tax increase for West Virginians. Recently Senator Manchin dismissed as trivial the roughly $750 to $1,000 dollars a year it will take from each West Virginia taxpayer, although that figure dwarfs the amount Manchin cut in taxes as governor and for which he loudly and often takes credit.

These contradictions must register somewhere in Senator Manchin's mind because he has resorted to a truly cynical defense of his vote claiming that an extension of the payroll tax cut "jeopardizes Social Security" by taking "hundreds of billions of dollars out of the funding stream". However, the Social Security law stipulates that, in the event of a deficit, funding is automatically supplemented from the government's general revenue fund making Social Security as stable as the rest of the government – a fact of which Manchin is aware if not forthcoming. So, again, why?

Since Manchin's arguments on both sides of the tax cut debate cancel each other out, it's hard to tell what his motives are. Maybe he's a rare soul who can simultaneously hold conflicting beliefs and who, like, Oscar Wilde, considers "a foolish consistency" to be "the hobgoblin of little minds". Or maybe he's a victim of "doublethink", the delusory state George Orwell's novel "1984" describes as a precursor to becoming a pawn of Big Brother. But whether guided by hobgoblins or Big Brother, Joe Manchin's actions on this issue are a mystery and a problem for West Virginia. ■

A PLEA FOR THOSE OF NO FAITH

February 29, 2012

This evening hundreds of thousands of West Virginians will sit down to dinner without saying grace and they and their children will go to bed without prayers. On Sunday morning, rather than go to church, they'll sleep late, enjoy a leisurely breakfast, read a newspaper, and relax with bottomless cups of tea or coffee. Others will rise early, not to worship God, but to take a walk or hike. And it's all good.

We're talking about non-religious West Virginians – secular West Virginians. A small number are atheists, some are agnostics, but mostly they're regular people, free of doctrine, for whom religious belief and practice simply aren't parts of their lives. They may or may not believe in God. They may or may not be spiritual. But they share a common characteristic in having little interest in religion because even without religious faith they're happy and fulfilled while in public life they're solid citizens and contributors to the general good.

That's not to say that all secular people are virtuous and happy. But, as we shall see, they seem to do at least as well as their religious counterparts and there are lots of them. According to recent studies by the Pew Forum on Religion and Public Life and the Gallup organization 29% of West Virginians and more than a third of Americans say religion is not an important part of their daily lives. About a fifth of West Virginians rarely or never attend church.

Secular Americans are spread out pretty much across the political spectrum, although they are somewhat less likely than the population as a whole to identify as Republicans. And you can't really blame them given the rhetoric of Republican presidential candidates.

"How can you have judgment if you have no faith? How can I trust you with power if you don't pray?" thunders Newt Gingrich who frequently cites secularism as America's greatest threat. In Rick Santorum's lexicon, the word "secular" is regularly associated with the excesses of the French Revolution, collapsing values, and various forms of totalitarianism. And Mitt Romney warns about the dangers of "the religion of secularism".

If you happen to be a secular American sitting at home watching TV and you hear this kind of vitriol and hysteria, you almost have to remind yourself that it's you they're talking about. Romney, Santorum, and Gingrich rail about a "war on religion", but you're the one who is being insulted to a degree and in terms that religious Americans never have to endure. But, as aggravating as that is, mostly you wonder just what it is these guys are talking about.

That's because, as the United States has become more secular, it's generally become a better place to live. Steve Chapman addressed this issue in a recent Chicago Tribune column.

"In the past couple of decades, most indicators of moral and social health have gotten better, not worse. Crime has plummeted. Teen pregnancy has declined by 39 percent. Abortion rates among adolescents are less than half of what they were. The incidence of divorce is down. As of 2007, 48 percent of high school students had engaged in sex, compared to 54 percent in 1991."

Then Chapman points out that the states that lead in these measures of quality of life far from being the most religiously observant are instead the least observant and most secular.

Vermont and New Hampshire, the states with the lowest rates of church attendance in the country have the fewest murders. Mississippi has the highest rate of church attendance in the country and one of the highest murder rates.

Chapman goes on. "Of the ten states with the most worshippers, all but one have higher than average homicide rates. Of the eleven states with the lowest church attendance, by contrast, ten have low homicide rates." The same dynamic is true of other measures of morality and social well-being.

Teen pregnancy rates are highest in states where religious observance is most prevalent and lowest where it is not. Divorce rates are very low in comparatively secular states such as Massachusetts and Connecticut, where same-sex civil unions are legal, but above average in the Bible belt and among adults who classify themselves as evangelical or "born again". Rates of crime, charitable giving, and volunteerism also show that in general more secular states do better than more religiously observant ones.

So, why do the Republican candidates fear and vilify secularism?

They don't trust it. They don't believe morality can exist in the absence of an active faith in God. None the less, they're contradicted every day by millions of Americans and hundreds of thousands of West Virginians who conduct virtuous lives grounding their morality, not in religious faith, but in the principles of love, compassion, duty, and charity – impulses they and almost all people feel spontaneously, impulses that don't diminish whether God is present in their lives or not.

If Gingrich, Santorum, and those who are of a like mind on issues of faith can set aside their rhetoric about secularism and take a look at whom secular Americans actually are and the lives they lead, they'll find great comfort and reassurance. Perhaps then they will politely respect these people who are, as much as any Americans, good parents, good neighbors, excellent citizens, and important contributors to what is good in West Virginia and America. ■

OFFICE OF FUDDERALISM

February 4, 2013

"At wast! The wong arm of the waw is weaching out and cwosing in on you, you scwewy wabbit." – Elmer Fudd

In this case, the long arm of the law is that of West Virginia Attorney General, Patrick Morrisey, and the "scwewy wabbit" isn't Bugs Bunny, but the federal government, which, in Mr. Morrisey's view, has a penchant for passing laws and issuing regulations that stifle economic growth, deprive us of freedom, and, at least sometimes, violate the Constitution.

So, Mr. Morrisey is establishing an Office of Federalism and Freedom and charging it with the task of "identifying and challenging unconstitutional laws and regulations". Mr. Morrisey has also made it clear where he's going to start looking – Obamacare, the Environmental Protection Agency, and any gun control measures that might emerge in the wake of the Sandy Hook tragedy. The effort will be led by attorney Elbert Lin, a former clerk of Supreme Court Justice, Clarence Thomas, and a member of the Federalist Society.

But, what is federalism?

The Constitution's 10th amendment reserves to the states or the people powers not expressly granted to the federal government. In that spirit, federalism is the principle that, to the degree practicable, power should devolve to governmental units nearest the people. Federalism is usually invoked by states that believe federal laws or regulations usurp their powers.

Although federalism was once cited in defense of slavery and is often associated with conservative causes, inherently it's neither conservative nor liberal. States have invoked federalism to defend liberal policies such as assisted suicide, medical marijuana, greenhouse gas regulations, and campaign finance reform. Here in West Virginia, when natural gas companies sued Morgantown over its ban on fracking, claiming that state law preempts municipal law, the city defended its ban on federalism grounds among others.

Federalism can also be taken to extremes. Texas Governor Rick Perry cited federalism when claiming that Social Security and Medicare are unconstitutional and recent Republican senate candidate, John Raese, wanted to abolish the EPA, the federal Department of Education, and the minimum wage on federalism grounds.

But, while politicians, usually Republicans, profess fealty to federalism, most do so opportunistically and set federalism aside when attempting to impose pet policies on unwilling states. Examples include congressional attempts to limit stem cell research and abortion, the No Child Left Behind Act, the federal Defense of Marriage Act, and nearly annual attempts to enact national medical malpractice reform.

In short, great mischief can be made both under the banner of federalism and in spite of it. Mr. Morrisey, a former congressional staffer turned lobbyist, seems an unlikely extremist, but political opportunism may be within his reach. Mr. Morrisey has earned the right to apply the principles on which he campaigned. But, if he applies federalism on a selective basis to achieve ideological goals that conservatives cannot achieve electorally and legislatively, the results won't be good. In fact, it won't even be Federalism. It will be Fudderalism.

Fudderalism, named for Elmer Fudd, the world's greatest practitioner of monomaniacal fixation ("Kill the wabbit!"), is characterized by a lack of moderation, objectivity, and rigor that usually ends in disaster.

Objectivity may prove challenging for Mr. Morrisey. Ideally the federalism office will select issues impartially rather than cherry-pick them in pursuit of a political agenda. But, Mr. Morrisey has already announced his intention to hit three conservative hot buttons – EPA regulations; Obamacare, notwithstanding the Supreme Court's ruling that the law is constitutional; and gun control, despite the fact that law he pledges to fight hasn't even been enacted. Meanwhile, Mr. Morrisey, who supports natural gas development, has been silent on the Morgantown fracking ban even though the principle of federalism suggests that Morgantown and not the state should decide the terms of development within municipal borders.

Another test of objectivity will be the reports and opinions produced by the new office. Will they focus narrowly on the legal questions at issue, carefully weighing the arguments for and against? Or will they read like campaign press releases designed to score political points with hyperbolic phrases such as "job killing"?

And how great will be their scope? Will they confine themselves to the legal merits of the laws in question or will they explore economic and social implications as well? If they adopt the broader perspective, how objectively and competently will they do it?

It's one thing to claim on the campaign trail that EPA regulations kill jobs, but reports issued by the Attorney General's office should meet higher standards. Claims should be substantiated and quantified and the underlying data made available so observers can verify the claims' validity. In that regard, Obamacare may pose a problem for the Attorney General because, ideological objections aside, the measure is extremely beneficial for West Virginia, insuring more than a hundred thousand currently uninsured residents and pumping hundreds of millions of dollars annually into the state's economy at very little cost, which is why Ohio Governor John Kasich decided his state should fully expand Medicaid under Obamacare despite his philosophical opposition.

So, will it be the Office of Federalism or Fudderalism? Will it adopt a non-partisan stance that examines laws impartially and reports on them objectively or will it become an ideologically driven, taxpayer funded, conservative propaganda mill?

So far, Mr. Morrisey has been "vewy, vewy quiet" on these questions. Let's hope it's not because he's already out there hunting wabbits. ∎

WEST VIRGINIA'S SCHOOL OF FARCE

November 19, 2012

"Farce is tragedy played at a thousand revolutions per minute." John Mortimer

It's tempting to treat the recent firing of West Virginia superintendent of schools, Dr. Jorea Marple, as farce because that's the form the characters and events seem to demand.

First, there is Board of Education president, Wade Linger, whose inept ouster of Marple violated nearly every principle of sound management.

You know you've failed as a leader when you end up looking worse than the person you fired. That's the spot in which Linger put himself and the Board because, whether Dr. Marple deserved to be fired or not, Linger provided neither warning nor reasons before taking action and his embarrassing inability or unwillingness to do so since makes the episode reek of backroom dealing and cronyism.

In ramrodding through of Marple's dismissal, Linger blatantly ignored the state's open meeting law as well as assorted personnel due process requirements and even failed to notify at least two other Board members of his intention to raise the issue. Then Linger burnished his reputation for arrogance by reminding those who dared question his actions that the superintendent serves at the pleasure of the Board. Otherwise, he offered only a few content-free platitudes about the need for a "new direction" before asserting that the board's priorities are to "build mutual trust", "commit to change and transparency", and "improve communication".

I'd give my right arm to know how the AP reporter who recorded those comments managed to keep a straight face.

Linger and his allies on the Board have succeeded only in plunging the state into crisis and opening the way for assorted lawsuits. They've also reminded us why our ineffectual Governor Earl Ray Tomblin always uses his middle name. Otherwise people might assume his middle initial stands for "ridiculous", which is how he appears after allowing days to go by without comment except for a prepared statement in which he feebly thanked Dr. Marple for her service, but said nothing about her firing.

By comparison, Virginia's governor, Bob McDonnell, was faced with a similar crisis earlier this year after the University of Virginia Board of Governors attempted to carry out a similar hit job on the president of that university. Faced with an uproar not unlike the one building in West Virginia, McDonnell threatened to fire the entire Board unless they resolved the issue while demanding, "Regardless of your decision, I expect you to make a clear, detailed and unified statement on the future leadership of the university."

"A clear, detailed and unified statement" is precisely what West Virginia's Board of Education has not given citizens of the state and, one suspects, cannot.

But Linger's ineptitude; Tomblin's ineffectuality; the tears we are told that Dr. Marple shed over her firing; the rumored political intrigues of former governor, Joe Manchin, who appointed the board members who voted for Marple's dismissal, and those of his wife, Gayle, who sits on the Board are just "Happenings in Hooterville", the ongoing soap opera that is our state capital. What we need to focus on are the kids and deciding what we need to do to improve upon West Virginia's standing as the least educated state in the nation.

At present there is no public discussion of these issues by the governor or members of the Board of Education. In fact, as he tries to ram through the appointment as state superintendent of Randolph County schools superintendent, James Phares, Board President Linger is working assiduously to ensure there is no discussion or debate lest it derail the appointment of a cipher whose views on educational policy are generally unknown.

Meanwhile, when asked about educational policy, the governor and others in state government point to the now almost legendary Educational Audit. But that document, whatever its merits, is about making schools more cost effective and not much about how to improve education. While saying a great deal about administration and expense management, the audit contains not a word about curriculum, teaching methods, and early childhood preparedness – all issues that West Virginia desperately needs to address.

Remarkably, as of this writing the governor and the Board of Education still have it within their power to snatch victory from the jaws of defeat. They can respond to the current fiasco by temporarily reinstating Dr. Marple, if she is willing, and by conducting a public review of her performance in which any criticisms or concerns that Board members have, as well as Dr. Marple's replies, are put on the table to be considered by all West Virginians. At the same time, other candidates for the job should be invited to submit credentials as well as their visions for education in West Virginia. These should also be shared publically. Such a process would allow West Virginia to initiate a much-needed public discussion and even salvage a shred of dignity.

Ironically, last year, when the Board conducted its most recent superintendent search from which Dr. Marple emerged as the unanimous selection, Board president Linger expressed dismay that there weren't more applicants from around the nation and he openly wondered why. He needn't have looked any farther than the mirror for an answer. After witnessing Linger's banana republic-like leadership of the Board, few qualified candidates are likely to apply for the opportunity to labor under the whimsical ways of West Virginia politics. But, what's done is done and we must muddle through as best we can. ∎

WEST VIRGINIA: TWO PARTIES, ONE IDEOLOGY

March 27, 2012

What are the differences in the positions of Governor Earl Ray Tomblin and Republican challenger, Bill Maloney, on taxes, economic development, coal and gas, the environment, healthcare, worker safety, abortion, and same-sex marriage?

The answer? There are no differences or, if differences exist, the men's positions are but a hair's breadth apart.

Both support tax reduction – particularly on businesses – as the primary strategy for economic development. Both oppose same-sex marriage and abortion. Both are strident advocates for coal and gas development. Both aggressively oppose the Environmental Protection Agency and question or deny the existence of man-made global warming. Both oppose most or all of Obamacare, with Tomblin pleading that his actions to implement the law are undertaken only because he is legally required to act. Neither supports worker safety protections, particularly in coal mining, beyond those mandated by the federal government.

In fact, the only discernible differences in the political postures of the two men are that Maloney fervently supports judicial reform, which Tomblin opposes, and Tomblin is an ally of unions, which Maloney generally opposes. But, even those differences have less to do with matters of principle than they have to do with whose supporters stand to gain or lose – trial attorneys and teachers for Tomblin and businesspeople and the Chamber of Commerce for Maloney.

It's pretty much one political ideology and two candidates whose primary interests lie in taking care of their own.

This sameness of ideology isn't confined to gubernatorial politics. After they win their parties' respective nominations, Senator Joe Manchin and Republican John Raese will compete again this fall for the US Senate. Raese will face the daunting challenge of finding issues on which he differs from Manchin. Once Raese thought he had openings on Obamacare and Cap and Trade legislation. But, Manchin took those away by announcing just prior to the last election that he had changed his position and would henceforth oppose Obamacare. Then he famously put a bullet through the Cap and Trade bill.

Sometimes the sameness of ideology in West Virginia is ironic. In the last election cycle, ethically challenged first district Democratic congressman, Alan Mollohan, lost his primary race to former state senator, Mike Oliverio. Mollohan tried to cast his opponent as a pawn of right wing interests because Oliverio was the West Virginia co-chair of the American Legislative Exchange Council (ALEC), a right-wing think tank funded by the archconservative Koch brothers and an assortment of corporations. Mollohan might have had a point since ALEC is the source of many highly conservative "model bills" that inspired the Wisconsin law attacking state employee collective bargaining rights;

voter ID laws that are accused of disenfranchising students, old people, and minorities; an assortment of measures designed to repeal Obamacare at the state level; and the "stand your ground law" made famous in Florida's Trayvon Martin case, which has also been enacted in West Virginia.

The effectiveness of Mollohan's accusation was blunted, however, by the fact that Oliverio's predecessor as the West Virginia chair of ALEC was one Joe Manchin. In true bipartisan spirit, the current West Virginia ALEC chair is Republican state Delegate and Tea Party favorite, Eric Householder. And ALEC's most enthusiastic supporter may be local Delegate Jonathan Miller who is challenging Republican Congresswoman Shelley Moore Capito from the right.

Even West Virginia news media are largely monochromatic. West Virginia MetroNews, content-provider to 57 radio stations statewide and home to the popular Hoppy Kercheval, is owned by the afore-mentioned senate candidate, John Raese, to whom Kercheval is a campaign contributor as well as an employee. Meanwhile, the state's largest newspaper chain, Ogden Publications, Inc., which owns the Journal in Martinsburg and five other daily newspapers in the West Virginia, is reliably conservative and pro-business in its editorial positions.

Taken together, West Virginia's political class is almost invariably allied with business interests and largely silent on issues that make West Virginia last in the nation in nearly every measure of well-being. We don't have Democrats and Republicans. We have an "Accommodationist Party" with two only slightly differentiated wings.

West Virginia is in dire need of new perspectives. We need voices that, instead of reflexively condemning Obamacare and ignoring the state's health crisis, will propose ways of achieving universal coverage and expanded access to care. We need voices addressing the state's lowest-in-the-nation level of educational attainment and proposing policies that will make advanced education and four-year degrees an expectation, if not inevitability, for all West Virginia students. We need voices pointing out that simple-minded tax cutting is a myopic, inadequate, and failed strategy for attracting investment to the state and that; instead, we must address shortcomings in infrastructure, workforce, and quality of life. We need voices demanding action on licit and illicit drug use, the associated rise in violent crime, and our dearth of prevention and treatment options. We need other voices pointing out that coal is a dying industry and that it along with natural gas, while having value, has not been, is not, and will never be a major engine of prosperity for West Virginia. And we need recognition that the coal industry, in its death throes, is cannibalizing the state economically and environmentally and that it has already shed 80% of the jobs it once provided and they aren't coming back.

But, in our homogenized political environment, these points go unmade and there is no debate. And we are the losers because of it. ■

CONFESSIONS OF A FROG

CONFESSIONS OF A FROG

October 4, 2012

The fellow was rambling on about how structural steel melts at 2,777 degrees, while jet fuel burns at 1,517 (Fahrenheit? Celsius? Who knows?). So, the planes couldn't have caused the World Trade Center to fall. Besides, the average velocity of 26.7 meters per second at which the towers collapsed could only have been achieved by means of thermite explosives detonating in rapid and choreographed succession. "Uncontestable facts!" he insisted.

I suspected he was wrong. But, being neither an engineer nor a chemist, I couldn't contest him. And, as a theater director, his authority was pretty wobbly too.

In short, we were two naïfs arguing an issue about which we knew nothing. If the situation sounds ridiculous, it was. But, arguing about things of which we know little isn't unusual. We do it in the pages of this newspaper, in coffee shops, over the dinner table. Economics, global warming, even our nation's history are topics we debate heatedly but with little expertise. And, as absurd as that may be, our political system empowers us in our ignorance to select leaders based on whether their only slightly better-informed opinions coincide with our own.

I don't say this to trash democracy, but to observe that the way in which we arrive at our positions and argue is a precarious business.

Recently an offended reader called me a glib charlatan and ridiculed my habit of citing "specious" statistics and historical precedents. I indignantly responded that the statistics are facts, my glibness is logic, and his rejection of history's lessons makes him incapable of rational discussion and consigns him to the hell of his preconceptions. Harsh stuff.

Actually, he's not that bad, nor am I as righteous as my indignation would like. But, the conflict I accused him of avoiding – the one between preconceptions and facts – is something with which we all struggle.

In a perfect world, facts would always win out and we would adjust our worldviews to accommodate them. But, it's not that easy.

Because our understanding of most issues is derivative, that is, based on the expertise of others – parents, teachers, authors, traditions – when a contradictory fact comes along, it may change our understanding of not just a particular event, but of many events and also discredit sources upon which we rely. Dominos start falling and our understanding begins to unravel.

If a threatened source is foundational in our lives, the unraveling can be so severe that we'll reject or ignore the disruptive facts. Doing so isn't always delusion or prejudice. Even the scientific method sometimes values order over fact. When confronted with two equally plausible explanations for a phenomenon, the explanation that is in greater accord with other accepted theories is preferred even if it fails to account for all the facts.

While facts are important, so is coherence and to prefer the latter to the former isn't always bad. But it can be.

In his book, "500 Days", Kurt Eichenwald reports that president George W. Bush said to a stunned French president Jacques Chirac of the war in Iraq, "This confrontation is willed by God, who wants to use this conflict to erase his people's enemies before a New Age begins".

The war, of course, descended into chaos accomplishing only a reshuffling of Iraq's sectarian deck at immense human, moral, and economic cost. The reasons for its undertaking – ostensibly the threat posed by weapons of mass destruction – and for its continued conduct over eight bloody years were constantly contradicted by facts, which the president apparently interpreted not as helpful input and as reasons to change course, but as deceptions designed to test his faith.

Bush's inability to adapt his worldview in response to facts is the opposite of the 9/11 conspiracy theorist theater director who allowed a few unexplained facts to undermine conventional understanding of an immensely complex event.

The point is that balancing facts against worldviews is necessary and hard. Intelligent people of good will can look at the same facts and interpret their meaning differently – something we should keep in mind when we find ourselves so dumbstruck by our opponents' blindness that we think it can only be the result of stupidity or evil intent.

And we can improve our ability to assimilate new facts through education.

Herodotus first noticed and social scientists confirm that those who are least informed tend to be the most intransigent in their opinions. That's because their knowledge is mostly derivative, consists of few facts, and comes from just a few sources. Consequently, new and contradictory facts can wipe out large parts of their worldviews in an instant. So, they resist. On the other hand, the better educated who have more detailed and nuanced understanding more easily assimilate new facts, even disruptive ones, and do so with less cognitive fallout.

If we can balance fact against coherence, we can be rational without being expert. That's important if we're to select good leaders and make good policy choices. We also need to accept the validity of other viewpoints because they're inevitable. The genius of democracy isn't that we always get it right, but rather that we all feel heard and are, therefore, willing to face the consequences of our choices, whether good or bad, together.

So, to the reader I accused of being incapable of rational discussion, I was wrong. My friend, you were called ugly by a frog. ∎

BLUTO AND THE TEA PARTY

August 24, 2012

Gee, I loved "Animal House". Do you remember when the Delts were facing expulsion from college and Bluto (John Belushi) rallied them with an impassioned speech?

D-DAY: War's over, man. Wormer dropped the big one.

BLUTO: Over? Did you say "over"? Nothing is over until we decide it is! Was it over when the Germans bombed Pearl Harbor? Hell no!

OTTER: [whispering] Germans?

BOON: Forget it, he's rolling.

I suppose we can overlook a lot when somebody's rolling. And that's just what I did when I recently had breakfast with a Republican candidate for West Virginia's house of delegates. During our conversation he mentioned that communism and fascism are really the same thing.

I let slide what I thought was an obvious inaccuracy because the comment was merely parenthetical and took place during a discussion of tax policy. But, in a strange coincidence, later that day a friend forwarded a 10-minute video titled "The American Form of Government". The Tea Party-inspired video described various political ideologies including communism, socialism, fascism, and Nazism and, like my breakfast companion, went on to explain they are all the same thing.

The claim that these ideologies or systems of government are the same raises two issues. First, it's patently wrong for reasons I'll explain in a moment. Second, why have the definitions of ideologies that are in some respects little more than historical artifacts acquired such consequence, at least to people with Tea Party leanings?

To understand the difference between communism and socialism, which are on the political left, and fascism and Nazism on the political right, let's turn to the late Jeane Kirkpatrick, former Georgetown University political science professor, a staunch anti-communist conservative, and President Ronald Reagan's ambassador to the United Nations.

One of Kirkpatrick's signature contributions to political science was her distinction between "totalitarian" governments on the one hand, which included the Soviet Union, Cuba, North Korea, China, and others; and "authoritarian" states on the other hand, which included Franco's Spain, the Shah's Iran, Marcos's Philippines, and Pinochet's Chile.

The difference she pointed out is that in totalitarian regimes governments are not only politically repressive, but they also collectivize the economy and own or control the means of production. Whereas authoritarian regimes, while they may be as politically repressive as their totalitarian counterparts, none-the-less allow the economy to remain largely in private hands.

For Kirkpatrick and other conservatives, that latter characteristic, the willingness of dictatorial regimes to tolerate free markets and private ownership, meant that, while we might regret their lack of political freedom, they still had shared interests with the United States and were, therefore, acceptable allies politically, economically and militarily.

Although Kirkpatrick's belief that the United States should ally with authoritarian regimes was and is debatable, her distinction was a valid one. And to prove it, one needs look no farther than Nazi Germany. Decades before the Nazis came to power, privately held companies such as Daimler-Benz, Bayer, and BMW were well established. They continued to be privately held during the Nazi period and throughout World War II and are still with us today.

The same point could be made for all of the other authoritarian regimes mentioned above, which unlike Nazi Germany, the United States considered to be allies. And, truth be told, prior to the United States' entry into World War II, even Nazi Germany was not universally reviled. Prominent Americans such as Henry Ford and Charles Lindbergh were favorably disposed toward Hitler and the Rockefellers' Standard Oil of New Jersey carried on a thriving business with the Nazi regime.

Also noteworthy is the fact that, while the United States has accommodated authoritarian dictators such as Marcos, Franco, and Pinochet; democratically elected leaders who nationalized or threatened to nationalize some industries, such as Iran's Mosaddeqh, the Shah's predecessor, or Salvador Allende who preceded Pinochet in Chile, fell victim to overthrows supported or even engineered by the United States.

In short, when the behavior of other countries brought into conflict two core American values – democratic government based on the consent of the governed and free enterprise – the United States willingly sacrificed the former in favor of the latter.

That's why, while Tea Party sympathizers are fearful of incipient socialism, their counterparts on the left are just as fearful of creeping fascism. Given American tolerance of non-democratic regimes, it's entirely plausible to those on the left that there are economically powerful people who would willingly undermine basic political freedoms in order to achieve political dominance and commercial advantage.

Whether deserved or not, that's the fear surrounding Charles and David Koch, the politically active brothers who heavily fund various right wing causes including the Tea Party.

But, regardless of whether anyone's fears are well-founded, why is it that, despite a bright line theoretical distinction between totalitarianism and authoritarianism and extensive historical examples, folks aligned with the Tea Party movement are at such pains to blur or even deny the distinction?

For some, it may be a case of ignorance, but for others who know better or should know better, there is reason to suspect a propagandistic attempt to bundle up the sum total of Americans' political fears and deposit them at their opponents' end of the political spectrum while making their own extremism seem pure, incorruptible, and risk free.

If true, it's a dangerous thing. After all, at the end of "Animal House" Bluto became a United States senator. One shudders to think. ∎

COMEDY & TRAGEDY WITH GUNS

February 19, 2013

Do you know how once you stub your toe it seems like you keep on banging it again and again, constantly reaggravating the injury? Since publishing an earlier column on gun violence and how the presence of guns increases the lethality of conflicts, especially those that arise within families and even within ourselves to produce horrific numbers of murders, suicides, and inevitably compound murder/suicides, I've been constantly reminded of the prevalence of gun-enabled horror by a seemingly unending stream of news stories, one of them funny, but the others tragic.

To keep things light, let's start with the funny one. It was recently revealed that the National Rifle Association maintains a Nixonian "enemies list", which, due to embarrassment, has since been removed from the organization's web site, but which has been helpfully recreated by Abby Zimet of Common Dreams. The list contains people and organizations the NRA considers to be "anti-gun". With over five hundred entries, the list features a "Who's Who" of celebrities and prominent groups who can be difficult to categorize, but it's fun to try.

Short people – Danny DeVito, Peter Dinklage, and Dustin Hoffman (Really. Hoffman is so short that while filming the movie "Rain Man" Tom Cruise, who stands all of 5' 7" used to say, "Thank God for Hoffman. Otherwise I'd be the last person to know when it rains.")

Divas – Gloria Estefan, Madonna, Beyonce, Shaka Khan, and Barry Manilow

Zappas – Dweezil, Ahmet, Moon Unit, and Diva (who could have been under "Divas", but family first!)

Won't make the Hall of Fame, but at least they got some recognition – pitcher Mike Torrez, quarterbacks Vinny Testaverde and Doug Flutie (who I nearly put in the "short people" category because, when lined up under center, he had to stand on this toes to see the defense. But, I decided to take mercy.)

West Virginians – Mary Lou Retton and Jennifer Garner (Now that this is out, will they be allowed back in the state to visit family?)

Women on whom I've had a crush – Meryl Streep, Diane Keaton, Helen Hunt, and Meg Ryan (pre-work)

Women on whom I haven't had a crush – Fran Drescher, Bette Midler, Penny Marshall, Rosie O'Donnell, and Meg Ryan (post-work)

The state of Missouri – An array of prominent businesses in the St. Louis and Kansas City areas including the phone company and, interestingly, every major league sports team in the state including the St. Louis Rams, the St. Louis Cardinals, and the Kansas City Chiefs (must be lingering resentment over the guns vs. bows and arrows mismatch).

People who have to deal with the tragedy – The National Association of Police Organizations, the National Association of School Safety and Law Enforcement Officers, and the Police Foundation

People who have to clean up the mess – Many medical organization including the American Medical Association, the American Association for the Surgery of Trauma, the American Academy of Pediatrics, and the American Nurses Association.

People who have to conduct the funerals – "American Jewish Committee, the Central Conference of American Rabbis, the Lutheran Office for Governmental Affairs, the United States Catholic Conference, the Congress of National Black Churches, the Episcopal Church's Washington Office, the Friends Committee on National Legislation, the United Methodist Church General Board & Church Society, and the United Church of Christ Office for Church in Society.

But, as funny or unfunny as the NRA's enemies list is, there has also been a steady drumbeat of gun-enabled tragedies involving prominent people who are united in having owned guns as a means of protection only to find their protective weapons turned on their loved ones, themselves, and often both.

The Greg Griego family – Greg Griego was a prominent minister in Albuquerque, New Mexico. In January, his fifteen year-old son, Nehemiah, apparently took a gun from the family collection and murdered Griego, his wife, and Griego's three daughters ages 9, 5, and 2.

The American Sniper – Chris Kyle, former military sniper and author of the best-selling memoir, "American Sniper", and a friend were apparently murdered by a fellow veteran who they had invited to a shooting event.

Oscar Pistorius – The famed Olympic athlete has been charged with shooting his girlfriend to death.

Mindy McCready's Boyfriend – David Wilson was found shot to death at singer Mindy McCready's home. The death was presumed to be a suicide, but police say the case is still open.

Mindy McCready – Apparently shot herself to death days after her boyfriend David Wilson was shot to death.

Dr. Bruce Foster and Marlise Foster – The prominent Charleston, WV doctor and his wife died from gunshot wounds in an apparent murder/suicide.

As I said, it's like the stubbed toe you just keep smacking again. Or maybe since writing about the horrific toll of gun violence I'm just more apt to notice these things. But, either way, it reminds me of the absurdity of owning a gun for self-protection. I just pray for those who do and, more than that, for their loved ones and friends that the ongoing litany of tragedies finally begins to penetrate their minds and souls so that they, their friends, and family members won't end up on this list that sadly is growing even faster than the NRA enemies list. ■

ABRAHAM LINCOLN, THE UNPRINCIPLED

November 9, 2012

(Christine Miller Ford of the Spirit of Jefferson, who was doing a column about the movie "Lincoln" asked for my thoughts on why Abraham Lincoln still fascinates us. This was my reply.)

I think Lincoln fascinates us as a president because he saved the United States and with it the promise of everything the founding fathers hoped for, everything this nation has become, and everything it might yet be.

But, I think he fascinates us even more as a human being. He, like you and I, had principles in which he believed, principles he articulated in order to be elected president. But, his principles were tested by as great a catastrophe as one person has ever faced – a conflict that resulted in the deaths of hundreds of thousands.

It would be nice to say that through it all Lincoln adhered to his principles and that's why he's a hero today. But, that's not what happened. He didn't adhere to his principles. He couldn't, at least not in the naïve form in which he imagined them before being elected president.

Lincoln was confronted by a situation so monstrous and complex that it constantly pitted treasured principles against one another forcing him to question them, to refine them, to choose between them, and occasionally sacrifice some of them.

By the standards of the day Lincoln was a dove, but he prosecuted the most destructive war in this nation's history. He wasn't an abolitionist, but he abolished slavery. He was a profound believer in republican democracy, but at times he assumed nearly dictatorial powers.

And despite all the painful compromises he had to make, Lincoln never tried to escape responsibility by taking either of the two backdoors through which many of us run. He didn't take shelter in dogma. He believed in God, but he knew his choices and the responsibility for the consequences were his alone.

And Lincoln never gave in to expediency. He might have been forced to sacrifice lesser principles in order to protect the most precious. But, he held on to those tightly.

In the end, I think Lincoln fascinates us because he reminds us that living is damned hard and too complex to allow all of our choices to be guided entirely by a few simple rules handed down in books, by our religion, or even by our parents. Eventually, we all face choices for which we cannot know what's best. And, at times like that, Lincoln's example is a comfort because it reminds us that, despite our inadequacy, we can still act conscientiously and even nobly. ■

ESSAY ON FAITH FOR "THIS I BELIEVE"

September 22, 2011

(The following essay was written for the "This I Believe" oral history program and was recorded on November 21, 2011 at Shepherd University.)

Last year while filling out a computer dating profile and trying to offset the truth conveyed by my pictures, which can be summarized as, "bald, middle-aged, pencil-neck geek", I experienced a small identity crisis. It happened when I came to the question about faith.

The options were generous – Baha'i, Buddhist, Christian Catholic, Christian Protestant, Jewish, Muslim, and others along with atheist, agnostic, and the ambiguous "spiritual but not religious", which sounded suspiciously like taking credit for believing without the responsibilities. Anyway, the question stopped me for two reasons. First, I was looking for a date and … well, you know. But, I bravely defeated the temptation to dissemble only to encounter a bigger problem – I didn't know what I was.

It wasn't for lack of consideration. After all, I was once a philosophy major and had even been confirmed in the Lutheran church. But that was never more than a formality for my parents or me.

We just weren't religious, which didn't mean there weren't occasional clerical encounters. Once while hitchhiking at age 14 I was picked up by a tent preacher who was holding a revival. He asked if I was a Christian and, being a precocious snot, I opined that I thought not because at the time I was reading Hugh Schonfield's book, "The Passover Plot" that purported to debunk the miracles of Jesus. The preacher gave me a dire look and said archly, "You know that book was written by a Jew!", his implied meaning eluding my adolescent understanding altogether. At about the same time, the reverend at the Lutheran church where I was confirmed (and had ever since been absent) showed up on our front porch expressing concern for my soul to my equally unconcerned mother. Otherwise, I've been pretty much religion-free and I suppose faith-free as well.

But, the question on the profile demanded an answer. Although I could have checked "Christian Protestant", it would have been hypocritical. And "atheist" was too dogmatic. Even "agnostic" missed the mark by suggesting a depth of contemplation about faith that far exceeded the amount I'd given it. For the truth is, thoughts of God and faith rarely cross my mind I suppose because their absence triggers no anxiety, creates no void, leaves no questions disturbingly unanswered.

Our understanding of the physics and biology of our world, although never completely settled, seems sufficient to me and, as important, moral principles such as love, compassion, duty, and charity are comfortable as well because I feel them spontaneously as I think all or at least most people do. And while I don't always agree with others about how those values should be interpreted and applied, I know we share a common impulse to nurture and care.

In that spiritual bond I comfortably place my trust.

So, in my dating profile I became "Spiritual but not religious", because, I realized, it confers all of the responsibilities even in the absence of belief. ∎

INDEX